STAAR Prep
Grade 8 Composition

by Suzanne E. Borner

Edited by Patricia F. Braccio

Item Code RAS2577 • Copyright © 2011 Queue, Inc.

Queue, Inc. • 80 Hathaway Drive • Stratford, CT 06615
(800) 232-2224 • Fax: (800) 775-2729 • www.qworkbooks.com

Table of Contents

A Review: Good Writing

Think about a time when you read something that you enjoyed. What made you want to keep reading? Your answer probably has something to do with good writing. This book will help you learn to recognize the elements of good writing so that you can use some of the same techniques to become a better writer yourself.

1.   PLANNING AND ORGANIZATION

A good composition has a clear beginning, middle, and end. The ideas are in the right order, they make sense, and they remain focused on the subject.

Prior to writing, however, it is a good idea for the writer to come up with a plan of action. Graphic organizers, outlines, and notes help a writer to brainstorm and to organize thoughts and ideas. Tools such as these are invaluable in helping a writer to get his or her thoughts together and to focus on the subject of the composition.

Next, it is important to decide how to present this information. Some writers begin their compositions with the most important information. Others prefer to save this until the end. Some writers discuss events in the order in which they occur or explain an idea in controlled steps while others present information in creative and zany ways. There are unlimited ways to present a topic. Deciding on this before beginning to write will help to save time.

2.   WAYS TO BEGIN A COMPOSITION

Perhaps the most important part of a good composition is the introduction because it is your first and only opportunity to hook your readers (grab their attention) and motivate them to keep reading. Here are just a few ideas about how you could effectively begin a composition:

- a compelling or surprising fact

- a thought-provoking question

- an interesting quotation

- a vivid description of an event

- a sentence that states the main idea or topic

- an opinion

- a statement addressed directly to the reader

3. PURPOSE AND AUDIENCE

A good writer knows exactly why he or she is writing a composition and for whom the composition is written. There are three primary types of writing:

- narrative or descriptive writing

- expository or informational writing

- persuasive writing

Each has a different purpose and audience:

A **narrative** composition tells a story following a plot that includes specific characters, a setting, an action, and a resolution.

An **expository** composition conveys information. It should include an introduction, which states the main idea; a body, which supports the main idea; and a conclusion, which sums up the main idea.

A **persuasive** composition attempts to persuade or convince readers to do or to believe something.

*NOTE: The best and most effective compositions often incorporate all three styles of writing.

4. STYLE, VOICE, AND TONE

Style is a technical term for the affect or mood a writer creates through the mechanics of the composition. Tone is the writer's attitude toward the subject. Voice is the person the audience hears in their minds as they read.

Closely related to purpose and audience, style, tone, and voice combine to form the overall feeling or emotion the audience experiences upon reading the composition. Is the essay serious or is it humorous? Is it casual or is it passionate? Is it formal or is it informal? Is it zany or is it controlled? Is it simple or is it full of details? The style, tone, and voice of the composition will answer these questions.

5. FOCUS: RELEVANCE AND REDUNDANCY

The material included in a good composition should be relevant to the topic. It should remain on-target, focused, and connected with the main idea and purpose of the writing. The writer should not include information that does not belong because that could confuse readers as well as take up valuable space.

A good composition also avoids redundancy. A writer should not repeat the same words, phrases, and ideas over and over. This detracts from the overall flow of the writing.

6. SENTENCES, PARAGRAPHS, AND TRANSITIONS

A good paragraph is well organized. It usually begins with a sentence that states the main idea of the paragraph and contains a number of supporting sentences. It is important to vary the length and tone of your sentences so that the composition does not become monotonous. Sentences should also be complete and well written. Finally, each paragraph usually ends with a sentence that wraps up or reiterates the information presented within it.

A good way to move from one idea to another in a composition is to use transition words or phrases. Transition words and phrases help to establish logical connections between sentences, paragraphs, and sections of your papers.

Some commonly used transition words include: also, however, on the other hand, on the contrary, next, afterward, of course, therefore, again, nevertheless, consequently, moreover, finally, and nonetheless.

7. INTERESTING AND DESCRIPTIVE WORDS / SUPPORTING DETAILS

A good composition uses interesting and descriptive words and details that help to describe the topic, as well as words that help to activate the senses. Good writing answers the questions **Who? What? Where? When? Why?** and **How?** Descriptive words and details help readers to get good pictures in their minds as they read. These details can help to make a composition much more interesting. Good details also include facts, statistics, logical reasoning, predictions, personal experiences, prior knowledge, and opinions that help to support the main idea.

Consider the following example:

> *It was not a very nice bus.*

This sentence is vague. It does not provide readers with any details that would show how, exactly, the bus is not nice. Consider the more descriptive rewrite:

> *The enormous yellow school bus was packed with screaming children. It smelled like old sneakers and there was something sticky on the faded green leather seat in the back row.*

This rewritten sentence contains many more interesting and descriptive details that help readers to get good pictures in their minds about why the bus is not nice.

8. CHARACTERS: DIALOGUE AND EMOTION

A good writer might decide to include characters in his or her composition. Through characters, the writer can incorporate dialogue and reveal emotion, both of which help to make a composition much more interesting to readers. Whether the composition is expository, narrative, or persuasive, the inclusion of characters who can deliver dialogue and emotion is a wonderful tool for writers who hope to engage and affect their readers.

Consider the following example:

He told me that he liked it.

This example does not give readers much of an idea about what is going on in the sentence. Consider the rewritten example:

He chewed the last bite slowly, savoring it. When he finally swallowed, a satisfied grin stretched from ear to ear. "That was the most delicious piece of hot apple pie I've ever eaten," he announced. Then he washed it down with a tall glass of milk.

This example helps readers to appreciate the character and the situation. It is filled with details that activate our senses and make us feel as though we're in the story, too.

9. WAYS TO END A COMPOSITION

A good composition has a strong and memorable conclusion. The purpose of your closing paragraph is to wrap things up and leave readers with a lasting impression of the topic. Here are just a few ideas of ways you could end a composition:

- Summarize or restate the main idea.

- Address the reader directly.

- Make a prediction or comment on the future.

- Express an opinion.

- Express a thought, feeling, or statement related to the main idea.

- Leave the reader wondering about an unanswered question.

To the Student: *The first assignment in this book is filled out for you. This example, on pages ix–xx, shows you how to complete most of the rest of the book.*

Example: Solar Eclipse

Avalon's English teacher asks her to write an expository composition in response to this prompt:

> What is a total solar eclipse? When does such a thing occur? How do you know when it is happening? How do you witness such an event? What is the difference between a solar eclipse and a lunar eclipse? Tell what you know about the phenomenon of a total solar eclipse.

Here is one of Avalon's drafts. Read it and then answer the questions that follow.

Avalon's Draft A

A total solar eclipse is a phenomenon that occurs when the moon passes between the earth and the sun. When the angle is just right, the moon can move directly in front of the sun, totally covering it. The complete eclipse, which <u>isn't even detectable</u> until the sun is ninety percent covered, lasts no more than seven minutes and that during this time, strange things happen. The sky may become as black as night. The temperature may drop twenty degrees. Confused birds and animals may act strange.

Though predictable, total solar eclipses are extremely rare. The last one visible to people in the United States occurred in 1991—in Hawaii. The next one that will be visible to people from locations within this country will not take place until 2017. However, this is no reason for those of you <u>intrigued by</u> this phenomenon to fret. There are two main types of eclipses: solar (of the sun) and lunar (of the moon). Both are very <u>interesting to astronomers</u>. Up to five types of solar eclipses occur each year somewhere in the world. There are usually three lunar eclipses annually as well, so that's plenty to choose from,

A lunar eclipse is different from a solar eclipse. In a lunar eclipse, Earth is in between the moon and the sun. The Earth temporarily blocks out the light of the sun so the moon gets covered in a shadow, which is the eclipse. A lunar eclipse can only occur when the moon is full, not when it's in the shape of a crescent or any other time. There are partial and total eclipses and they are both safe to watch with the naked eye. The most recent lunar occurred on October 28, 2004, during Game 4 of the World Series. Some say that it why the Red Sox won for the first time in 86 years! Indeed, strange things are believed to happen during eclipses and that is definitely one of them!

However, back to solar eclipses, which are definitely more exciting because when else does day become night? Remember, if you ever get the chance to witness a solar eclipse, be very careful. Don't be fooled into thinking that just because the sun is blocked, you can watch this whole incredible phenomenon with your bare eyes. You may not realize it, but the sun is still <u>emitting dangerous rays</u> during this time. These can cause

(continued on next page)

(continued from previous page)

severe damage to your eyes, and even blindness. When the date of a solar eclipse is approaching, take the advice of the experts by making a pinhole camera or wearing special solar glasses. Or instead, just sit back and enjoy the show—without looking up. Feel the instantaneous drop in temperature. Observe how birds and animals begin to act. Notice how much like nighttime it has become.

Sometimes I like to imagine what I would have done if I lived back in the days of early humans? Back then, there would have been no technology. There would have been no scientists or astronomers to explain things to the people. Imagine how frightening it must have been to witness an eclipse—especially a solar eclipse? I wonder how people reacted. What did they do? Did they think the world was going to end? Did they think that the sun was disappearing forever? Did they think that they were being punished for something they did? I think it's fascinating to imagine stuff like this. Even though we'll never know, it's really incredible to think about it or to make up stories about it.

I don't think that I would have freaked out or panicked if it were me. I think I just would have been <u>fascinated by the whole phenomenon</u> as it was happening. I probably would have tried to look at the sun for too long, because I would not have known any better. I wonder how many people have gone blind by staring at a solar eclipse. It would be extremely interesting to find out the answer to that one.

1. How does the writer begin the composition?

    _____ a compelling or surprising fact

    _____ a thought-provoking question

    _____ an interesting quotation

    _____ a vivid description of an event

    _√_ a sentence that states the main idea or topic

    _____ an opinion

    _____ a statement addressed directly to the reader

    _____ other _____

2. What is the main idea of the composition?

    The main idea of this composition is what solar and lunar eclipses are and how we can observe them. (Remember, however, that the prompt asked Avalon to write about solar eclipses only!)

x

3. What are three details that support the main idea in this composition?

    The writer explains exactly what solar and lunar eclipses are and how to observe

    them. She also wonders how early man would have reacted to seeing such a

    phenomenal event.

4. Is there any information that does not belong in this draft?

    Information about lunar eclipses and the time one occurred during a World Series

    game do not belong in this draft.

5. Descriptive details are details that help readers to get good pictures in their minds as they read. Underline five descriptive details in this draft.

6. A good composition has a clear beginning, middle, and end. Number the paragraphs in order as they occur. Tell which numbers are beginning paragraphs, which are middle paragraphs, and which are ending paragraphs.

    Paragraph 1 is an introduction. Paragraphs 2–6 are middle, supporting paragraphs.

    There is no clearly-defined concluding paragraph.

7. How does the writer end the composition?

    _____   summarizes or restates the main idea

    _____   addresses the reader directly

    __✓__   makes a prediction or comments on the future

    _____   expresses an opinion

    _____   expresses a thought, feeling, or statement related to the main idea

    _____   leaves the reader wondering about an unanswered question

    _____   other _____

Here is Avalon's other draft. Read it and then answer the questions that follow.

Avalon's Draft B

Imagine for a moment that it is 5,000 years ago. You live among a group of hunters and gatherers. You take shelter and sleep in caves. You communicate by body language and monosyllabic sounds. Technology is thousands of years in the future.

One afternoon, just as you are starting off for a hunt, something odd starts to happen. You look up to see that the <u>sky is darkening</u>, as if night were coming on. The sun is disappearing! You try to watch, but it burns your eyes to look. Confused and afraid, you run as fast as you can back to the cave where you find the other members of your tribe huddled in the depths, <u>shaking, crying, and praying</u> to the gods to stop the coming destruction. You join them; you're all sure that this is the end.

After a few hours, when nothing extraordinary has occurred and you realize that you're still alive, you decide to venture back outside. You can't believe your eyes. Things are back to normal. The sun is shining bright and hot on the <u>grassy plains</u>, as if nothing had ever happened. You run back into the cave to inform your tribe that the gods have been merciful.

You could never have known that what you and your fellow tribesmen experienced that day was a <u>celestial phenomenon</u> known to modern civilization as a "total solar eclipse." Thankfully, we now understand that eclipses of any sort are nothing to fear. On the contrary, they are to be admired and studied. There are two main types of eclipses: "solar" (of the sun) and "lunar" (of the moon). Although both are very interesting to astronomers, solar eclipses are much more exciting for the rest of us. When else does day turn into night?

The phenomenon of the total solar eclipse stopped being considered such a <u>frightening and mysterious event</u> approximately 2,500 years ago, when many ancient civilizations began to realize what was actually happening. As they discovered, a total solar eclipse occurs when the moon passes between the earth and the sun. When the angle is just right, the moon can move directly in front of the sun, totally blocking it. The eclipse, which isn't even detectable until the sun is ninety percent covered, lasts no more than seven minutes. During this time, strange things happen. The sky may become as black as night. The temperature may drop twenty degrees. Confused birds and animals may act strangely.

Though predictable, total solar eclipses are extremely rare. The last one visible to people in the United States occurred in 1991—in Hawaii. The next one that will be visible to people from locations within this country will not take place until the year 2017. However, this is no reason for those of you intrigued by this phenomenon to fret. Up to five other types of solar eclipses occur each year somewhere in the world, and there are usually three lunar eclipses annually as well.

However, remember: If you ever get the chance to witness a solar eclipse, be very careful. Don't be fooled into thinking that just because the sun is blocked, you can watch this whole incredible phenomenon with your bare eyes. You may not realize it, but the sun is still emitting dangerous rays during this time. These can cause severe damage to your eyes, and perhaps even blindness. When the date of a solar eclipse is approaching,

(continued on next page)

(continued from previous page)

take the advice of the experts by making a pinhole camera or wearing special solar glasses. Or, instead, just sit back and enjoy the show—without looking up. Feel the instantaneous drop in temperature. Observe how birds and animals begin to act. Notice how much like nighttime the day has suddenly become.

However you choose to witness a solar eclipse, enjoy it. It might be a long time before you see another one.

8. How does the writer begin the composition?

_____ a compelling or surprising fact

_____ a thought-provoking question

_____ an interesting quotation

_✓_ a vivid description of an event

_____ a sentence that states the main idea or topic

_____ an opinion

_____ a statement addressed directly to the reader

_____ other _____

9. What is the main idea of the composition?

The main idea of this composition is what a total solar eclipse is.

_____

_____

_____

10. What are three details that support the main idea in this composition?

The writer gives the definition of a solar eclipse, explains how to safely witness

one, and tells us when the next one will occur in the United States (the year 2017).

_____

_____

11. Is there any information that does not belong in this draft?

    There is no information that does not belong in this draft.

    _____

    _____

    _____

12. Descriptive details are details that help readers to get good pictures in their minds as they read. Underline five descriptive details in this draft.

13. A good composition has a clear beginning, middle, and end. Number the paragraphs in order as they occur. Tell which numbers are beginning paragraphs, which are middle paragraphs, and which are ending paragraphs.

    Paragraphs 1—4 are introductory paragraphs. Paragraphs 5—7 are middle,

    supporting paragraphs. Paragraph 8 is the conclusion.

    _____

14. How does the writer end the composition?

    _____ summarizes or restates the main idea

    _____ addresses the reader directly

    __✓__ makes a prediction or comments on the future

    _____ expresses an opinion

    _____ expresses a thought, feeling, or statement related to the main idea

    _____ leaves the reader wondering about an unanswered question

    _____ other _____

15. You have now read two drafts of Avalon's work. One is her rough draft, and one is an improved draft.

    Which do you think is the improved draft?   Draft A _____   Draft B __✓__

16. Tell why you chose this draft.

    Draft B is the improved draft because it starts by building on an idea the writer

    presented at the very end of Draft A where she vividly described what it would have

    been like for early man to witness a solar eclipse. This will grab and hold the

    attention of readers and inspire them to continue reading. The writer then goes on

    to provide excellent and relevant information about solar eclipses. In Draft A, on

    the other hand, the writer gets off-target by including too much information about

    lunar eclipses. It also lacks an outstanding introduction and conclusion.

17. What are three other possible titles for this composition?

    Students should be encouraged to come up with creative and unique ideas for other

    possible titles.

Now it's your turn. Write an expository composition in response to this prompt and then answer the questions that follow.

Choose any celestial event and write a composition about it. Explain to your readers what it is. Is it a phenomenon? How and why does this event happen? How often and when does it happen? Can human beings witness it? Tell everything you know about this particular event.

AS YOU WRITE YOUR COMPOSITION, REMEMBER TO:

- Begin the composition with a topic sentence.

- Choose at least three details to support your topic sentence.

- End with an idea that restates or pulls together the main topic or idea.

1. How do you begin your composition?

   _____   a compelling or surprising fact

   _____   a thought-provoking question

   _____   an interesting quotation

   _____   a vivid description of an event

   _____   a sentence that states the main idea or topic

   _____   an opinion

   _____   a statement addressed directly to the reader

   _____   other _____

2. What is the main idea of your composition?

   _____

   _____

   _____

   _____

   _____

3. What are three details that you use to support your main idea?

   _____

   _____

   _____

   _____

   _____

4. Does your composition have a clear beginning, middle, and end?

   Yes _____   No _____

5. Write down three examples of descriptive or interesting details that you used in your composition.

_____

_____

_____

_____

6. What do you want your readers to learn from reading this composition?

_____

_____

_____

_____

7. How do you end your composition?

_____ summarize or restate the main idea

_____ address the reader directly

_____ make a prediction or comment on the future

_____ express an opinion

_____ express a thought, feeling, or statement related to the main idea

_____ leave the reader wondering about an unanswered question

_____ other _____

8. What are three possible titles for your composition?

_____

_____

_____

To the Student: Now it's your turn. Read the assignments carefully and answer all the questions. Then practice what you have learned by writing your own compositions. Use your imagination and be creative. You are on your way to becoming a better writer.

Topic 1:   Running Out of Gas

Michael's English teacher asks him to write an expository composition in response to this prompt:

> Someday in the future, the world's supply of fossil fuel will run out. That means no gasoline to fuel our cars. As a society that relies on fuel-powered vehicles, how are we going to handle this problem? Explain what people are doing now in order to prepare for the day when we no longer have enough fuel for our cars and trucks. Tell what you know about coping with or even solving this potential problem.

Here is one of Michael's drafts. Read it and then answer the questions that follow.

Michael's Draft A

In the future, when we run out of gasoline, that will be good in some ways because it won't pollute the air so much. It will also be bad in some ways because it would be hard to get around. People are working on making new kinds of cars that run on different stuff. My friend's dad has a hybrid car. Also, my uncle said that he is going to buy one of them. Lots of car companies are now making hybrid cars. So there are a lot to choose from I think that they are a great idea. I don't know why my parents don't have one and probably I will talk to them about this.

What I would do is a few things. First of all, I would start walking or riding my bike to as many places as I could. I would stop waiting for and demanding rides from everyone. Especially if someplace is really close like school, or town, or the library, there is no good reason for me to go there in a car. That is a waste of gas and gas is really expensive. Plus we need more exercise around here so this would make us get up and get more exercise. I can understand it when it's winter and cold or rainy, but there's no excuse for not walking or riding your bike when it's nice out and the place is close.

Another thing I would do is tell all the adults I know to buy a car like the hybrid car. The kind of car I always wanted though, was a Hummer. Unfortunately, those are really gigantic and they use a lot of gasoline so they are probably not to good to have. Plus they are very expensive. They go through gas so fast too, that you are probably always going to be stopping at the gas station. I don't have that kind of money. And then, what happens when the world runs out of gas? I'd be stuck with a big old Hummer in the yard. It would make a good tank to play in with my friends, I guess.

(continued on next page)

1

(continued from previous page)

I want to be a soldier someday because I think they are very brave. They get to drive around in things like Hummers and defend our country. Without soldiers, we might not still be the United States of America today.

Another thing I could do is to decide to stay closer to home after school and on the weekends. If you have the choice between driving ninety miles to go to an amusement park and staying home and going to the movies, maybe for a while anyway, it would be better to just stay home. That way. We won't waste a lot of gas. That makes sense. And maybe someday, somebody will find extra fuel somewhere in the world, but until then we should be really careful and try to conserve everything that we do have.

1. How does the writer begin the composition?

    _____   a compelling or surprising fact

    _____   a thought-provoking question

    _____   an interesting quotation

    _____   a vivid description of an event

    _____   a sentence that states the main idea or topic

    _____   an opinion

    _____   a statement addressed directly to the reader

    _____   other _____

2. What is the main idea of the composition?

    _____

    _____

    _____

    _____

3. What are three supporting details in this composition?

    _____

    _____

    _____

    _____

2

4. A good composition has a clear beginning, middle, and end. Number the paragraphs in order as they occur. Tell which numbers are beginning paragraphs, which are middle paragraphs, and which are ending paragraphs.

    _____

    _____

    _____

5. Is there any information that does not belong in this draft?

    _____

    _____

    _____

    _____

6. According to the writer, what is a hybrid car?

    _____

    _____

    _____

    _____

7. A good writer tries to avoid run-on and incomplete sentences. If there are any examples of run-on or incomplete sentences in this draft, write them here.

    _____

    _____

    _____

    _____

8. How does the writer end the composition?

_____ summarizes or restates the main idea

_____ addresses the reader directly

_____ makes a prediction or comments on the future

_____ expresses an opinion

_____ expresses a thought, feeling, or statement related to the main idea

_____ leaves the reader wondering about an unanswered question

_____ other _____

Here is Michael's other draft. Read it and then answer the questions that follow.

Michael's Draft B

Just ask anyone who drives a car and the person will tell you that gasoline prices are staggeringly high and that they keep going up. Prices at the tanks have doubled and, in some cases, even tripled in the last decade. To make matters even worse, oil experts believe that, at the rate we are using it up, the world's supply of fossil fuels, which includes gasoline, will last for no more than fifty years.

Countries in Europe and Asia recognized this problem decades ago. As a result, the people there have been driving more environmentally-friendly, fuel-efficient cars for years. Yet, here in the United States, we continue to demand bigger cars, trucks, and sports utility vehicles (SUVs) with bigger gas tanks and more powerful engines that guzzle up to hundreds of thousands of gallons of fuel each day. Despite all the warnings out there, you can't drive down any highway in this country without seeing a large number of these vehicles.

Thankfully, there are people working hard to create cars that use alternative types of fuel. This means that, when gasoline runs out, we will be prepared. One of the most popular of these vehicles is a car called a "hybrid." A hybrid is a cross between a regular fuel-powered car and an electric car. The electric power in the hybrid means that it requires less gasoline to run. Driving this type of car not only helps to conserve the dwindling supply of fuel, it also helps to decrease the amount of pollution in the air.

Ideas for other types of alternative cars are in the works as well. In fact, fully electric cars have been around for more than one hundred years. However, because they run solely on battery-powered electricity, these cars must be charged and recharged continuously in order to continue working. Also, electric vehicles do not provide much power for climbing hills or traveling at higher speeds, so they have not yet gained in mass popularity.

The vehicle that is expected to become the car of the future is the hydrogen-powered car. This car combines hydrogen gas with oxygen to produce electricity. These

(continued on next page)

(continued from previous page)

cars will be as powerful as gasoline-powered vehicles, and they will never have to be charged like electric cars. Hydrogen would be cheaper and more readily available than gasoline, and it would give off far less pollution. Hydrogen cars are in the works already, and people could be driving them in just a few years.

The future is assured: gasoline will run out. It's just a matter of time before that happens. In the meantime, it's important to start conserving what little is left, and also to start preparing for a changing future. Don't leave it to the nation's automakers and inventors to come up with the ideas. Start thinking of your own. You never know, it could be you who comes up with the best idea yet for the car of the future.

9. How does the writer begin the composition?

_____ a compelling or surprising fact

_____ a thought-provoking question

_____ an interesting quotation

_____ a vivid description of an event

_____ a sentence that states the main idea or topic

_____ an opinion

_____ a statement addressed directly to the reader

_____ other _____

10. What is the main idea of the composition?

_____

_____

_____

_____

11. What are three supporting details in this composition?

_____

_____

_____

_____

12. A good composition has a clear beginning, middle, and end. Number the paragraphs in order as they occur. Tell which numbers are beginning paragraphs, which are middle paragraphs, and which are ending paragraphs.

_____

_____

_____

13. According to the writer, why is it a problem that Americans continue to drive gas-guzzling cars, trucks, and SUVs?

_____

_____

_____

_____

14. Is there any information that does not belong in this draft?

_____

_____

_____

_____

15. A good writer tries to avoid run-on and incomplete sentences. If there are any examples of run-on or incomplete sentences in this draft, write them here.

_____

_____

_____

_____

16. How does the writer end the composition?

_____ summarizes or restates the main idea

_____ addresses the reader directly

_____ makes a prediction or comments on the future

_____ expresses an opinion

_____ expresses a thought, feeling, or statement related to the main idea

_____ leaves the reader wondering about an unanswered question

_____ other _____

17. You have now read two drafts of Michael's work. One is his rough draft, and one is an improved draft.

Which do you think is the improved draft?   Draft A _____   Draft B _____

18. Tell why you chose this draft.

_____

_____

_____

_____

_____

_____

_____

_____

_____

_____

_____

19. Rewrite and improve the following sentence:

   Things the way we know them to be now are going to be changed big time in the coming years because our natural resources are going to go away.

   _____

   _____

   _____

   _____

20. What are three other possible titles for this composition?

   _____

   _____

   _____

   _____

   _____

   _____

   _____

8

Now it's your turn. Write an expository composition in response to this prompt and then answer the questions that follow.

Think about how air travel will change in the next one hundred years. Get an image in your mind of the airplane of the future. Now describe it. How big or small is it? How many passengers can ride in it at one time? Who pilots this plane? How fast does it go? To where can it travel? How expensive is it to travel this way? Is it better or worse than present-day airplanes? In what ways is it better? In what ways is it worse?

AS YOU WRITE YOUR COMPOSITION, REMEMBER TO:

- Begin the composition with a topic sentence.

- Choose at least three details to support your topic sentence.

- End with an idea that restates or pulls together the main topic or idea.

_____

_____

_____

_____

_____

_____

_____

_____

_____

_____

_____

11

1. How do you begin your composition?

   _____ a compelling or surprising fact

   _____ a thought-provoking question

   _____ an interesting quotation

   _____ a vivid description of an event

   _____ a sentence that states the main idea or topic

   _____ an opinion

   _____ a statement addressed directly to the reader

   _____ other _____

2. What is the main idea of your composition?

   _____

   _____

   _____

   _____

   _____

3. What are three details that you use to support your main idea?

   _____

   _____

   _____

   _____

   _____

4. Does your composition have a clear beginning, middle, and end?

   Yes _____   No _____

12

5. Write down three examples of descriptive or interesting details that you used in your composition.

    _____

    _____

    _____

    _____

    _____

6. What do you want your readers to learn from reading this composition?

    _____

    _____

    _____

    _____

    _____

7. How do you end your composition?

    _____ summarize or restate the main idea

    _____ address the reader directly

    _____ make a prediction or comment on the future

    _____ express an opinion

    _____ express a thought, feeling, or statement related to the main idea

    _____ leave the reader wondering about an unanswered question

    _____ other _____

8. What are three possible titles for your composition?

    _____

    _____

    _____

Topic 2:   Anxiety

Tariq's English teacher asks him to write an expository composition in response to this prompt:

> Anxiety is the feeling of distress, apprehension, worry, or uneasiness that we all experience from time to time, especially as we get older and begin to have more responsibilities. Think about your personal experiences with anxiety. What sorts of situations could cause you to feel anxious? Describe the physical sensations that anxiety might cause. How can you prevent anxiety from getting out of control or lasting too long? Tell what you know about anxiety from your experience, observations, and/or studies.

Here is one of Tariq's drafts. Read it and then answer the questions that follow.

Tariq's Draft A

You are next in line to deliver a speech for English class. Palms sweating and heart racing, you struggle to breathe. Your head is dizzy, spinning—so clouded and heavy that you can't hear what the student ahead of you is saying. His lips are moving but you hear nothing. You are sure that you can't even move, let alone stand up in front of the class to speak. You are resigned to the fact that paramedics will have to carry you out of school on a stretcher. This will be embarrassing, but better than having to do this speech, to be sure. When the teacher calls your name, however, you somehow manage to stand up, walk to the front of the class, and recite your speech from the note cards you spent hours preparing. The other students applaud when you finish and a calming relief washes over you as you collapse into your seat.

Anxiety is something that we all experience from time to time. Even though it's not the most comfortable feeling in the world, it's a natural and important part of being human, and none of us would want to be living without it. Thousands of years ago, ancient man relied upon feelings of anxiety for survival. The "fight or flight" mechanism was activated in times of perceived danger. This mechanism was the internal alarm that went off to notify man of trouble. In ancient times, however, the "fight or flight" mechanism was usually in response to real danger in a true life-or-death situation.

Obviously, things have changed. Most of us no longer run the risk of being attacked by saber-toothed tigers or tribes of cannibals. We do, however, experience other types of distressful situations that cause our "fight or flight" mechanisms to activate, like having to stand up in front of the class to deliver a speech. Even though this is not generally considered a dangerous activity, your body does not know the difference. Instead it detects your increasing anxiety and prepares you to cope with it. So, just as if

(continued on next page)

14

(continued from previous page)

your life were in grave danger, your heart begins to race, you sweat, your mind clouds over, and you feel frozen in place. However, this type of anxiety usually subsides shortly.

In times of prolonged stress, on the other hand, such as when there is a serious illness or a death in the family, or when you have a heavy workload, we can experience constant and persistent anxiety that just seems to go on and on. Think about what it might feel like if the anxiety you were feeling before that speech never, ever subsided—that all day, every day, your heart raced, your mind was clouded, and you felt paralyzed with fear. This is what it can feel like when anxiety overstays its welcome. It can be agonizing. In these cases, it is imperative that we learn and practice ways to try to alleviate it. Exercising regularly helps. So does practicing deep breathing, meditation, and other such relaxation techniques. Then, once our body gets a break from being stuck in that "fight or flight" mode, we regain the strength and energy we need to take on the next challenge.

Remember that anxiety is a natural and important part of life. However, no matter what the reason is that your "fight or flight" mechanism kicks in, just be sure not to let it kick around too long.

1. How does the writer begin the composition?

    _____ a compelling or surprising fact

    _____ a thought-provoking question

    _____ an interesting quotation

    _____ a vivid description of an event

    _____ a sentence that states the main idea or topic

    _____ an opinion

    _____ a statement addressed directly to the reader

    _____ other _____

2. On a scale from 1 to 10, with 10 being the best, how would you rate the introduction of this draft? Tell why.

    _____

    _____

    _____

    _____

3. What is the main idea of the composition?

_____

_____

_____

_____

4. What are some details that the writer uses to support the main idea in this
    composition?

_____

_____

_____

_____

5. Does the writer use any humor in this draft?   Yes _____   No _____

    If yes, give an example of his use of humor.

_____

_____

_____

_____

6. A good composition has a clear beginning, middle, and end. Number the paragraphs
    in order as they occur. Tell which numbers are beginning paragraphs, which are
    middle paragraphs, and which are ending paragraphs.

_____

_____

_____

7. Is this composition well organized and easy to follow?   Yes _____   No _____

8. Descriptive details are details that help readers to get good pictures in their minds as they read. Underline five descriptive details in this draft.

9. How does the writer end the composition?

_____ summarizes or restates the main idea

_____ addresses the reader directly

_____ makes a prediction or comments on the future

_____ expresses an opinion

_____ expresses a thought, feeling, or statement related to the main idea

_____ leaves the reader wondering about an unanswered question

_____ other _____

Here is Tariq's other draft. Read it and then answer the questions that follow.

Tariq's Draft B

Anxiety is kind of like fear. Anxiety is something that we all experience from time to time. A lot of different scenarios and situations can cause us to feel anxiety. One is doing a speech at school in front of the whole class. A lot of people do not like standing up in front of people. They do not like to be the center of attention. They do not like to have to talk or do anything in front of an audience. So if they have to for a class assignment, some people might seriously have a hard time with it. They might almost feel as though they cannot do it at all, like they're locked into their seats. I have felt that way before. Have you?

I don't know how some people do it who do it all the time or who don't mind doing it. I suppose they would have other anxieties that I don't though because everybody has different ones. Other things that people can be anxious about at school are taking tests, talking to people that intimidate them, getting called to the principal's office, and being late or missing the bus.

In the days of ancient man, thousands of years ago, ancient man had anxiety just like we do today. In those days, it was a really good thing that they had their anxiety because they needed it. It helped them to know when there was danger. Having anxiety helped them to prepare for coping with the dangers of the time. When the anxiety subsided, they knew the danger was over and they could go back to their daily business. So, you see, it was really important.

The anxiety that we have today is the same anxiety that they had. It's just that now we don't really have a many real and good reasons to have it, yet we still have it for less dangerous reasons. Like giving a speech, or taking a test. Only our body doesn't know the difference. Our body is still pretty much the same that it was thousands of years ago. The thing that's the hardest to cope with is that sometimes in this day and

(continued on next page)

(continued from previous page)

age, we can have anxiety that doesn't go away. It can persist and stay with us every day. This is hard to cope with because it's such an uncomfortable feeling to have and when it never seems to go away it can be really, really hard to deal with.

Even though it's not the most comfortable feeling in the world, it's a natural and important part of being human, and none of us would want to live without it because like I said before, it helps us to cope with things, no matter how dangerous or not.

When you are a child, you usually have less anxiety than you do when you are older. Not all the time. Some kids have a lot of it. Usually it's older ones though because older kids and adults have more stresses and things to worry about. The worse is when stress comes and stays. To have that feeling of stress for a long, prolonged time is tough to cope with. It's physically and mentally hard and almost hurts. It can also cause other problems like we can get sick, we can get ulcers, we can break out, we can have stomach problems, etc.

However, the best and really, the only good way to deal with anxiety is to try to relax and there are plenty of ways to do that. Can you figure out what they are?

10. How does the writer begin the composition?

_____   a compelling or surprising fact

_____   a thought-provoking question

_____   an interesting quotation

_____   a vivid description of an event

_____   a sentence that states the main idea or topic

_____   an opinion

_____   a statement addressed directly to the reader

_____   other _____

11. On a scale from 1 to 10, with 10 being the best, how would you rate the introduction of this draft? Tell why.

_____

_____

_____

_____

12. What is the main idea of the composition?

_____

_____

_____

_____

13. What are some details that the writer uses to support the main idea in this composition?

_____

_____

_____

14. Does the writer use any humor in this draft?   Yes _____   No _____

If yes, give an example of his use of humor.

_____

_____

_____

_____

15. A good composition has a clear beginning, middle, and end. Number the paragraphs in order as they occur. Tell which numbers are beginning paragraphs, which are middle paragraphs, and which are ending paragraphs.

_____

_____

_____

16. Is this composition well organized and easy to follow?   Yes _____   No _____

17. Descriptive details are details that help readers to get good pictures in their minds as they read. Underline five descriptive details in this draft.

18. How does the writer end the composition?

_____ summarizes or restates the main idea

_____ addresses the reader directly

_____ makes a prediction or comments on the future

_____ expresses an opinion

_____ expresses a thought, feeling, or statement related to the main idea

_____ leaves the reader wondering about an unanswered question

_____ other _____

19. You have now read two drafts of Tariq's work. One is his rough draft, and one is an improved draft.

Which do you think is the improved draft?   Draft A _____   Draft B _____

20. Tell why you chose this draft.

_____

_____

_____

_____

_____

_____

_____

_____

_____

21. How do you think the use of humor helps to make a composition on anxiety more interesting to read?

_____

_____

_____

_____

_____

_____

_____

_____

22. Write what you think might be a good, alternative ending to the improved draft.

_____

_____

_____

_____

_____

_____

_____

_____

Now it's your turn. Write an expository composition in response to this prompt and then answer the questions that follow.

> What is stress? What sorts of things cause stress? Who gets stressed? How should people cope with stress? Begin your composition with a descriptive scenario that helps your readers to better understand what stress is.

AS YOU WRITE YOUR COMPOSITION, REMEMBER TO:

- Begin the composition with a topic sentence.

- Choose at least three details to support your topic sentence.

- End with an idea that restates or pulls together the main topic or idea.

1. How do you begin your composition?

    _____ a compelling or surprising fact

    _____ a thought-provoking question

    _____ an interesting quotation

    _____ a vivid description of an event

    _____ a sentence that states the main idea or topic

    _____ an opinion

    _____ a statement addressed directly to the reader

    _____ other _____

2. What is the main idea of your composition?

    _____

    _____

    _____

    _____

    _____

3. What are three details that you use to support your main idea?

    _____

    _____

    _____

    _____

    _____

4. Does your composition have a clear beginning, middle, and end?

    Yes _____   No _____

5. Write down three examples of descriptive or interesting details that you used in your composition.

_____

_____

_____

_____

_____

6. What do you want your readers to learn from reading this composition?

_____

_____

_____

_____

_____

7. How do you end your composition?

_____ summarize or restate the main idea

_____ address the reader directly

_____ make a prediction or comment on the future

_____ express an opinion

_____ express a thought, feeling, or statement related to the main idea

_____ leave the reader wondering about an unanswered question

_____ other _____

8. What are three possible titles for your composition?

_____

_____

_____

Monique's English teacher asks her to write an expository composition in response to this prompt:

> In his "State of the Union" address in 2002, President George Bush put out a plea to all Americans. What did he ask of us and why? How can students answer his call? What would the result be if every citizen were to do as the president has asked?

Here is one of Monique's drafts. Read it and then answer the questions that follow.

Monique's Draft A

In his first "State of the Union" speech after the terrorist attacks of September 11, 2001, President George W. Bush took the opportunity to reach out to Americans by issuing a national call to service. In this, he encouraged all countrymen and women to involve themselves in the task of strengthening and improving our nation. He urged each and every one of us to dedicate two years, or 4,000 hours, over the course of a lifetime to community service. How many hours have *you* logged so far?

The idea is simple, but ingenious. If each individual citizen of the United States contributes a portion of his or her time to help those in need, the country as a whole will benefit tremendously. It's a tall order though. In recent years, we have become a nation of people inclined to stay home on our couches eating pizza and watching reruns of our favorite television shows or playing the latest popular video games. How many of us ever involve ourselves in the goings-on in our communities? Well, now is the time to see how much more fulfilling it can be to help people in need than to help yourself to another bowl of ice cream.

If you are interested in responding to the request of our commander-in-chief, and if you would like to contribute your time to the cause but have no idea of how to begin, there is a perfect starting point. The Freedom Corps was established in response to President Bush's call to service. It is an organization that helps Americans to find volunteer opportunities that match their interests and talents. The Freedom Corps is easily accessible on the Internet. Just go to its website, type in your zip code and many of the local volunteer opportunities will pop up. Then, just take your pick.

As teenagers, we are at the perfect age and time to try volunteer service. At this point in our lives, we probably have many different ideas about what we might like to do when we're grown. Volunteering can help us to test out certain potential interests. Are you interested in medicine or nursing? Then volunteer your time at a local hospital. Are you interested in working with children? Then sign up as a mentor, be an after-school tutor, spend a few hours at the local Boys and Girls Club. Do you enjoy helping

(continued on next page)

(continued from previous page)

senior citizens? Then visit the residents of a nursing home and spend a few leisurely hours listening to their passionate tales about the olden days.

There's no end to the possibilities. Perhaps you are interested in computers and technology. Well, there's always a need for volunteers at the library to instruct newcomers in the basics. Do you enjoy cooking? Make a huge quantity of lasagna or meat loaf for your local soup kitchen and spend a Saturday afternoon serving it up. Donate your time to the Salvation Army, the United Way, or to other types of agencies that provide people with the items that they need to get by. Join a turkey drive at Thanksgiving, or a toy drive during the winter holidays.

The important thing is that you get out there and see just how much your skills and talents are needed. If you do, you'll inevitably see the impact that you can make on your community in just a few hours of time. There's no good reason not to take action and there's no time like the present to do it. Not only will you be helping others, you'll be doing your part in answering our president's call to service. And, who knows, you might just find that you like it!

1. How does the writer begin the composition?

   _____ a compelling or surprising fact

   _____ a thought-provoking question

   _____ an interesting quotation

   _____ a vivid description of an event

   _____ a sentence that states the main idea or topic

   _____ an opinion

   _____ a statement addressed directly to the reader

   _____ other _____

2. What is the main idea of the composition?

   _____

   _____

   _____

   _____

3. What are three details that support the main idea in this composition?

_____

_____

_____

_____

4. A good composition has a clear beginning, middle, and end. Number the paragraphs in order as they occur. Tell which numbers are beginning paragraphs, which are middle paragraphs, and which are ending paragraphs.

_____

_____

_____

5. The following sentence appears in this draft:

    *The idea is simple, but **ingenious**.*

   What does the word *ingenious* mean?
   a. easy and basic
   b. original and clever
   c. expensive and extravagant
   d. complex and difficult

6. Why do you think the author considers the call to service an "ingenious" idea?

_____

_____

_____

_____

7. According to the writer, what is the Freedom Corps?

_____

_____

_____

_____

8. How does the writer end the composition?

_____   summarizes or restates the main idea

_____   addresses the reader directly

_____   makes a prediction or comments on the future

_____   expresses an opinion

_____   expresses a thought, feeling, or statement related to the main idea

_____   leaves the reader wondering about an unanswered question

_____   other _____

Here is Monique's other draft. Read it and then answer the questions that follow.

Monique's Draft B

> The State of the Union address is the speech in the month of January when the current president of the United States presents a speech to the people of the country. Usually he does this from the capital building, which is the famous building where all sorts of governing by governors and senators in our country takes place. It is usually televised and also put on the radio. Of course, back in the olden days, it probably wasn't on the television because there were no televisions until they were finally invented. Usually, all the main stations cover the speech. They all find a place and turn on to televise the thing live right when it's time to get started. Usually, the speech is made in the nighttime and usually take the place of a television show or two. It's only once a year, so it's not that much of an inconvenience. Also, it's sometimes quite interesting to hear what the president has to say.
>
> The President delivers various speeches all the time, all over the world, to all different audiences. However, the big ones are the State of the Union, which I have already mentioned, the inaugural address, which is his first speech after he becomes president, and that is all I can think of. Periodically, the president might give the nation other speeches if he needs to communicate something to us. He did that after 9/11 and he did that before the war in Iraq.

(continued on next page)

30

(continued from previous page)

Another type of speech the president gives regularly is his weekly radio address, which my dad listens to, but which I have not. I'm not even sure when it comes on or on what channel that it comes on. In any of his speeches, the president can talk to the people of the country. He can ask them to do things. He can encourage them. He can make them feel better. He can explain why he has decided to do something. He can tell about what's going on with other countries. It is good that he can communicate like this to us because it makes us feel more secure. Imagine if we never even saw or heard the president or had no idea what he was doing? We would have no trust in him whatsoever.

Regardless of whether you or your parents like whoever the president is at the time, we have to all at least be grateful that he communicates information to us and helps us to feel like we're an important part of things—because we are!

In that speech in 2002, the president wanted us to get more involved in our country. He asked us to get more involved. Volunteer, help each other. Work. I know a lot of people who are doing that. A lot of people were doing that before, but a lot of other people started doing it after 2002. I'm just not sure what exactly I could do to help out in the country so I'm not really doing anything. But when I'm older, I guess I could definitely do more, because at that point, I'll have a job and maybe a car and a family. Actually, I might not have too much time at that point. Maybe now would be the best time. I only wish I knew what to do.

So I think that when you're stumped as to what to do, you could do some research. Ask your teacher, or get on the Internet. Ask your parents. Read the newspaper. Go to the library. You might get ideas that way. There are definitely a lot of people in the country that need help. I would like to be able to help.

9. How does the writer begin the composition?

_____ a compelling or surprising fact

_____ a thought-provoking question

_____ an interesting quotation

_____ a vivid description of an event

_____ a sentence that states the main idea or topic

_____ an opinion

_____ a statement addressed directly to the reader

_____ other _____

10. What is the main idea of the composition?

_____

_____

_____

_____

11. A good composition has a clear beginning, middle, and end. Number the paragraphs
in order as they occur. Tell which numbers are beginning paragraphs, which are
middle paragraphs, and which are ending paragraphs.

_____

_____

_____

_____

12. What are three details that support the main idea in this composition?

_____

_____

_____

_____

13. According to the writer, what is the "State of the Union" Address?

_____

_____

_____

_____

32

14. According to the writer, what did the president say in his 2002 "State of the Union" speech?

_____

_____

_____

15. How does the writer end the composition?

_____   summarizes or restates the main idea

_____   addresses the reader directly

_____   makes a prediction or comments on the future

_____   expresses an opinion

_____   expresses a thought, feeling, or statement related to the main idea

_____   leaves the reader wondering about an unanswered question

_____   other _____

16. You have now read two drafts of Monique's work. One is her rough draft, and one is an improved draft.

    Which do you think is the improved draft?   Draft A _____   Draft B _____

17. Tell why you chose this draft.

_____

_____

_____

_____

_____

_____

_____

_____

18. Rewrite and improve the following sentence.

   The state of the union speech is the speech that the president of the united states speaks every single year to tell about how things are here.

   _____

   _____

   _____

   _____

   _____

19. What are three other possible titles for this composition?

   _____

   _____

   _____

   _____

   _____

   _____

   _____

   _____

Now it's your turn. Write an expository composition in response to this prompt and then answer the questions that follow.

When an emergency occurs, the people of a community often come together to help each other. If there was a terrible flood in your town but your own home was unaffected, what are some of the things that you and your family could do to help other individuals affected and afflicted by this disaster?

AS YOU WRITE YOUR COMPOSITION, REMEMBER TO:

- Begin the composition with a topic sentence.

- Choose at least three details to support your topic sentence.

- End with an idea that restates or pulls together the main topic or idea.

1. How do you begin your composition?

_____ a compelling or surprising fact

_____ a thought-provoking question

_____ an interesting quotation

_____ a vivid description of an event

_____ a sentence that states the main idea or topic

_____ an opinion

_____ a statement addressed directly to the reader

_____ other _____

2. What is the main idea of your composition?

_____

_____

_____

_____

3. What are three details that you use to support your main idea?

_____

_____

_____

_____

4. Does your composition have a clear beginning, middle, and end?

Yes _____   No _____

38

5. Write down three examples of descriptive or interesting details that you used in your composition.

_____

_____

_____

_____

_____

6. What do you want your readers to learn from reading this composition?

_____

_____

_____

_____

_____

7. How do you end your composition?

_____ summarize or restate the main idea

_____ address the reader directly

_____ make a prediction or comment on the future

_____ express an opinion

_____ express a thought, feeling, or statement related to the main idea

_____ leave the reader wondering about an unanswered question

_____ other _____

8. What are three possible titles for your composition?

_____

_____

_____

Topic 4: Appreciation

Shea's English teacher asks her to write an expository composition in response to this prompt:

What does it mean to appreciate something? What is the importance of having appreciation? Tell what the consequences of not having appreciation might be. Tell how all of us could benefit if more people were appreciative of the things that we have in our lives. Use descriptive examples to help explain what appreciation is and why it is important.

Here is one of Shea's drafts. Read it and then answer the questions that follow.

Shea's Draft A

Picture a typical child in a room full of toys and games. That child will naturally want to play with everything all at once. He'll start with one toy, then throw it aside the minute he gets bored, and move on to the next thing that grabs his attention. He'll leave piles of discarded toys in his wake, not really appreciating any single one of them. It's not his fault—there are just too many. He's on toy-overload!

It seems that too many of us nowadays are in the same predicament as this child. We see more things, bigger things, better things—and we want it all! Society has become so driven by the desire for all things bigger, faster, and better, that we seem to have forgotten how to appreciate what we DO have. Instead, we're caught up in the never-ending cycle of wanting more of everything. More, more, MORE! What we have is never enough; we're never satisfied. It's a horrible reality that none of us would like to admit being guilty of, yet we all are.

There is no disputing that the United States is a country of abundance and plentitude. We've got everything we need at our fingertips. Yet, is anybody satisfied with this? Does anybody ever stop to think about how fortunate we are to have so much? Not even close. If you get a computer, you're disappointed when a newer model comes out a month later. If your parents still have dial-up Internet when everybody else seems to have high-speed Internet, you are upset with them. If your mom buys you a brand new pair of sneakers, but they're not what everybody else is wearing, you might hide them in the back of your closet. You decide that your Range Rover isn't big enough so you get a Hummer. Twenty television channels aren't enough so you buy digital television with its hundreds of choices. Waiting ten minutes for a meal at a restaurant seems too long. Then, when the meal comes, you complain that the portion is too small, even though it's enough to feed four adults.

Why is this? What has happened to make us so demanding, so greedy, and so ungrateful? I suggest that we are not remembering and practicing the importance of

(continued on next page)

(continued from previous page)

appreciation. Appreciation is a hugely important and wonderful character trait that all of us could stand to have more of. To appreciate something helps us to replace those negative and destructive feelings of jealousy and greed that can creep in. Appreciation helps us to keep life in perspective and to remember the things that are really important. It helps us to remember how lucky we are to have what we have—how little or how much that might be.

So the next time that you don't get what you want for your birthday, don't be upset. Instead, be appreciative for the presents that you do get. Be appreciative that you are lucky enough to turn another year older. Be appreciative for your friends and your family. Be appreciative of everything that you have, for every moment that you have it.

1. How does the writer begin the composition?

   _____ a compelling or surprising fact

   _____ a thought-provoking question

   _____ an interesting quotation

   _____ a vivid description of an event

   _____ a sentence that states the main idea or topic

   _____ an opinion

   _____ a statement addressed directly to the reader

   _____ other _____

2. What is the main idea of the composition?

   _____

   _____

   _____

   _____

3. Is this composition well organized and easy to follow?   Yes _____   No _____

4. What are some details that support the main idea in this composition?

_____

_____

_____

_____

5. A good writer tries to avoid run-on and incomplete sentences. If there are any examples of run-on or incomplete sentences in this draft, write them here.

_____

_____

_____

6. A good composition has a clear beginning, middle, and end. Number the paragraphs in order as they occur. Tell which numbers are beginning paragraphs, which are middle paragraphs, and which are ending paragraphs.

_____

_____

_____

7. On a scale from 1 to 10, with 10 being the best, how would you rate this draft? Tell why.

_____

_____

_____

8. How does the writer end the composition?

_____ summarizes or restates the main idea

_____ addresses the reader directly

_____ makes a prediction or comments on the future

_____ expresses an opinion

_____ expresses a thought, feeling, or statement related to the main idea

_____ leaves the reader wondering about an unanswered question

_____ other _____

Here is Shea's other draft. Read it and then answer the questions that follow.

Shea's Draft B

In some places, some people don't have enough food. They are starving to death. In some places. Kids don't have toys or anything. No books, no school. Definitely no restaurants and malls. SUVs and TEVO. No nothing. They are poverty-stricken and struggling, here in this country too. Not just in other parts of the world.

We live in a society that in some places is so driven by the desire for all things bigger, faster, and better, that we do not really ever really appreciate what we have . Instead, we want more of everything. We always just want more. What we have is never seeming to be enough we're never seeming to be satisfied. We are so lucky to have so much and we do not even realize it. It's a horrible reality that none of us would like to admit we're guilty of. We all are. There is no disputeing that the U.S.A. is a county of abundance and a country of not appreciating.

We've got everything we need at our fingertips. Yet, is anybody satisfied with this? Does anybody ever stop to think about how fortunate we are to have so much? No. Instead, we continue to expect immediate access to whatever we need, the moment that we need it. We continue to demand the best, the biggest, and the most stylish of things. Why is this? What has happened to make us so demanding, so greedy, and so ungrateful?

The only answer I can come up with is that we are not being taught to appreciate what we have. Think of a typical child put in a room full of toys and games. That child will naturally want to play with everything at once; children are innately inclined to this and do not know any better. He'll start with one toy, then throw it aside the minute he gets bored and move on to the next thing that grabs his attention. He'll leave piles of discarded toys in his wake. He won't appreciate a single one of them. It's not his fault— there are just too many. He desperately needs his parents, his teachers, and the other adults in his life to teach him to appreciate, to respect, and to be grateful for these items. If they don't, he'll throw away things as an adult as quickly as he is doing as a child.

(continued on next page)

(continued from previous page)

> It seems that too many of us nowadays are just like this child. We keep demanding more things, better things. Learning appreciation takes away from the need to continuously want more. It takes away from the tendency to compare ourselves to others. Having appreciation takes the place of jealousy and insignificance. It helps to boost our self-esteem and helps us to have greater respect for others. Learning appreciation is the key to turning things around. It's better than not being appreciative.

9. How does the writer begin the composition?

_____ a compelling or surprising fact

_____ a thought-provoking question

_____ an interesting quotation

_____ a vivid description of an event

_____ a sentence that states the main idea or topic

_____ an opinion

_____ a statement addressed directly to the reader

_____ other _____

10. What is the main idea of the composition?

_____

_____

_____

_____

11. Is this composition well organized and easy to follow?   Yes _____   No _____

12. What are some details that support the main idea in this composition?

_____

_____

_____

_____

13. A good writer tries to avoid run-on and incomplete sentences. If there are any examples of run-on or incomplete sentences in this draft, write them here.

_____

_____

_____

_____

14. A good composition has a clear beginning, middle, and end. Number the paragraphs in order as they occur. Tell which numbers are beginning paragraphs, which are middle paragraphs, and which are ending paragraphs.

_____

_____

_____

15. On a scale from 1 to 10, with 10 being the best, how would you rate this draft?

_____

_____

_____

_____

16. How does the writer end the composition?

_____ summarizes or restates the main idea

_____ addresses the reader directly

_____ makes a prediction or comments on the future

_____ expresses an opinion

_____ expresses a thought, feeling, or statement related to the main idea

_____ leaves the reader wondering about an unanswered question

_____ other _____

17. You have now read two drafts of Shea's work. One is the rough draft, and one is an improved draft.

Which do you think is the improved draft?   Draft A _____   Draft B _____

18. Tell why you chose this draft.

_____

_____

_____

_____

_____

_____

19. Rewrite and improve the following sentence:

There is no disputeing that in the U.S.A. is a county of abundance.

_____

_____

_____

_____

20. In your own words, describe what *appreciation* is.

_____

_____

_____

_____

_____

Now it's your turn. Write an expository composition in response to this prompt and then answer the questions that follow.

What is praise? What is the important of giving praise to one another? If praise is withheld from someone, how might that negatively affect that person? Is there such a thing as too much praise? Can anyone give praise, or is it only for adults? Tell what you know about praise and the impact that it can have on human beings.

AS YOU WRITE YOUR COMPOSITION, REMEMBER TO:

- Begin the composition with a topic sentence.

- Choose at least three details to support your topic sentence.

- End with an idea that restates or pulls together the main topic or idea.

1. How do you begin your composition?

    _____   a compelling or surprising fact

    _____   a thought-provoking question

    _____   an interesting quotation

    _____   a vivid description of an event

    _____   a sentence that states the main idea or topic

    _____   an opinion

    _____   a statement addressed directly to the reader

    _____   other _____

2. What is the main idea of your composition?

    _____

    _____

    _____

    _____

    _____

3. What are three details that you use to support your main idea?

    _____

    _____

    _____

    _____

    _____

4. Does your composition have a clear beginning, middle, and end?

    Yes _____   No _____

50

5. Write down three examples of descriptive or interesting details that you used in your composition.

_____

_____

_____

_____

_____

6. What do you want your readers to learn from reading this composition?

_____

_____

_____

_____

_____

7. How do you end your composition?

_____ summarize or restate the main idea

_____ address the reader directly

_____ make a prediction or comment on the future

_____ express an opinion

_____ express a thought, feeling, or statement related to the main idea

_____ leave the reader wondering about an unanswered question

_____ other _____

8. What are three possible titles for your composition?

_____

_____

_____

Topic 5:   Aborigine

Adam's English teacher asks him to write an expository composition in response to this prompt:

> Who are the Aborigines? Where do they live? What is their history and their culture? What are their beliefs? Tell what you know about these people.

Here is one of Adam's drafts. Read it and then answer questions that follow.

Adam's Draft A

In recent decades, the government of Australia began to recognize the importance of their country's people. The Aboriginal Land Rights Act of 1976 ensured tribes that no more land would be taken from them. In addition, the tribes have also been given plenty of civil and equal rights. Despite the measures that have been taken to try to salvage their culture. Despite their unique and wonderful cultural history, this number continues to decline. There are definitely not as many of them as there were one hundred or two hundred years ago.

The Aborigine people of Australia are one with the land. Their ancestors are the rocks, rivers, and vegetation all around them. Therefore, these native people of Australia are most comfortable living off the land, and they have done so for thousands of years, living off the land. They are hunters and gatherers. The environment will provide them with whatever whenever. They don't want things like clothes, shoes, houses, or cars—such things as those that none of us could not do without. They don't have electricity or cell phones or other modern stuff. They are just like they were back in their past. Many Aborigine tribes move around and stay in a place for awhile and then move around some more.

The Aborigine tribes of Australia have art and culture too. Since they have no language, tribes have told stories to pass down stories over the generations. Legends too. Customs and traditions get passed on this way only. Many tribe people can do sculpting, painting bark and rocks, and beadworking. Another unique piece of the Aborigine culture is a didgeridoo. It's an instrument. It's long. It's made of bamboo or cane. The outer part is carved into designs it makes a low, vibrating hum. The didjeridoo, most often played in formal ceremonies such as funerals, makes a low, vibrating, humming sound.

Nowadays, tourists can hear the music, or buy the art of the Aborigine people on the streets of Australian cities. They can even buy compact discs too. This is really good for tourists who want to buy things, but not very good at all for the Aborigines. Although it goes against their beliefs and customs, many tribe members have forced into city areas to sell their stuff. They have been left with no other choice and that is solely because they must support themselves and their families. Everybody has to do that. You can't blame them for doing what they have to do it's just very sad.

(continued on next page)

52

(continued from previous page)

They have a rocky and difficult past. Ever since the Europeans began settling in Australia in the late 1700s, Aborigines died off. They got sick, they lost land, and they simply kept dying off until there weren't very many more left. This is like what happened in the United States to the Native Americans when the people began to go over there. It's a similar story.

The Aborigines are the native people of Australia. It is believed that they migrated there from somewhere in Asia more than fifty thousand years ago. They live in various tribes throughout the country. Despite the differences in languages and customs from tribe to tribe, there are three common bonds that most of them share: spiritual beliefs, art and culture, and a stormy history. These are the ties that bind the dwindling populations of the Aborigine people.

1. How does the writer begin the composition?

    _____   a compelling or surprising fact

    _____   a thought-provoking question

    _____   an interesting quotation

    _____   a vivid description of an event

    _____   a sentence that states the main idea or topic

    _____   an opinion

    _____   a statement addressed directly to the reader

    _____   other _____

2. What is the main idea of the composition?

    _____

    _____

    _____

    _____

    _____

    _____

3. Descriptive details are details that help readers to get good pictures in their minds as they read. Underline five descriptive details in this draft.

53

4. What are three details that support the main idea in this composition?

_____

_____

_____

_____

5. A good composition has a clear beginning, middle, and end. Number the paragraphs in order as they occur. Tell which numbers are beginning paragraphs, which are middle paragraphs, and which are ending paragraphs.

_____

_____

_____

_____

_____

6. Is this composition well organized and easy to follow?   Yes _____   No _____
Tell why or why not.

_____

_____

_____

_____

7. A good writer tries to avoid run-on and incomplete sentences. If there are any examples of run-on or incomplete sentences in this draft, write them here.

_____

_____

_____

_____

8. How does the writer end the composition?

_____ summarizes or restates the main idea

_____ addresses the reader directly

_____ makes a prediction or comments on the future

_____ expresses an opinion

_____ expresses a thought, feeling, or statement related to the main idea

_____ leaves the reader wondering about an unanswered question

_____ other _____

Here is Adam's other draft. Read it and then answer the questions that follow.

Adam's Draft B

The Aborigines are the native people of Australia. It is believed that they migrated there from somewhere in Asia more than fifty thousand years ago. They live in various tribes throughout the country. Despite the differences in languages and customs from tribe to tribe, there are three common bonds that most of them share: spiritual beliefs, art and culture, and a stormy history. These are the ties that bind the dwindling populations of the Aborigine people.

The Aborigine people of Australia believe strongly that they are one with the land. They believe that their ancestors are a physical part of the land. They believe that the spirits of their forefathers reside in the rocks, rivers, and vegetation all around them. The native people of Australia are most comfortable living off the land, and they have done so for thousands of years. They are hunters and gatherers. A peaceful and spiritual people, they believe that the environment will provide them with whatever they need, whenever they need it. They have no desires for material items such as clothing, shoes, houses, or cars—items that many of us could not do without. Many Aborigine tribes simply move from place to place, settling temporarily in one location until they are ready to move on again.

Another common bond between the Aborigine tribes of Australia is their art and culture. Since they have had no official written language, tribes have relied upon and mastered the art of storytelling to pass down stories, traditions, and legends. Many tribes are also talented in sculpting, painting bark and rocks, and beadwork. Another unique piece of the Aborigine culture is a musical instrument called the "didgeridoo." This five-foot-long wind instrument is typically carved out of bamboo or cane. The outer part is often carved with beautiful designs. The didgeridoo, most often played in formal ceremonies such as funerals, makes a low, vibrating, humming sound.

Nowadays, tourists can hear the music or buy the art of the Aborigine people on the streets of Australian cities. This is fortunate for curious tourists, but not fortunate

(continued on next page)

(continued from previous page)

at all for the Aborigines. Although it goes against their beliefs and customs, many tribe members have been forced into urban areas to sell their traditional products. They have been left with no other choice. They must support themselves and their families.

The last common tie among the native cultures is their rocky and difficult past. Ever since the Europeans began settling in Australia in the late 1700s, the population of Aborigines has declined. Forced to move into smaller and less desirable areas of the land and exposed to new European diseases, many tribes began to die off. Some became extinct. Members moved into the cities and began to assimilate into the white culture. In recent decades the government of Australia has finally begun to recognize the importance of their country's first people. The Aboriginal Land Rights Act of 1976 ensured tribes that no more land would be taken from them. In addition, the tribes have also been granted civil and equal rights.

Despite the measures that have been taken to try to salvage their culture, full-blooded Aborigines make up only about one percent of the population of the country. Despite their unique and wonderful cultural history, this number continues to decline. What the future holds for the Australian Aborigines is anybody's guess.

9. How does the writer begin the composition?

_____ a compelling or surprising fact

_____ a thought-provoking question

_____ an interesting quotation

_____ a vivid description of an event

_____ a sentence that states the main idea or topic

_____ an opinion

_____ a statement addressed directly to the reader

_____ other _____

10. What is the main idea of the composition?

_____

_____

_____

_____

_____

_____

11. What are three details that support the main idea in this composition?

_____

_____

_____

_____

12. A good composition has a clear beginning, middle, and end. Number the paragraphs in order as they occur. Tell which numbers are beginning paragraphs, which are middle paragraphs, and which are ending paragraphs.

_____

_____

_____

13. Descriptive details are details that help readers to get good pictures in their minds as they read. Underline five descriptive details in this draft.

14. Is this composition well organized and easy to follow?   Yes _____   No _____

Tell why or why not.

_____

_____

_____

_____

15. A good writer tries to avoid run-on and incomplete sentences. If there are any examples of run-on or incomplete sentences in this draft, write them here.

_____

_____

_____

_____

57

16. How does the writer end the composition?

     _____   summarizes or restates the main idea

     _____   addresses the reader directly

     _____   makes a prediction or comments on the future

     _____   expresses an opinion

     _____   expresses a thought, feeling, or statement related to the main idea

     _____   leaves the reader wondering about an unanswered question

     _____   other _____

17. You have now read two drafts of Adam's work. One is his rough draft, and one is an improved draft.

Which do you think is the improved draft?   Draft A _____   Draft B _____

18. Tell why you chose this draft.

_____

_____

_____

_____

_____

_____

19. Rewrite and improve the following sentence:

They don't want things like clothes, shoes, houses, or cars—such things as those that none of us could not do without.

_____

_____

_____

_____

58

Now it's your turn. Write an expository composition in response to this prompt and then answer the questions that follow.

> The indigenous people of the United States are the Native Americans. They have experienced a tumultuous history similar to that of the Australian Aborigines. What is the history of the Native Americans? How is their situation similar to that of the Aborigine people? What is being done nowadays to help Native Americans to maintain their culture, their land, and their traditions? Write what you know about the Native Americans of the United States of America.

AS YOU WRITE YOUR COMPOSITION, REMEMBER TO:

- Begin the composition with a topic sentence.

- Choose at least three details to support your topic sentence.

- End with an idea that restates or pulls together the main topic or idea.

_____

_____

_____

_____

_____

_____

_____

_____

_____

_____

_____

1. How do you begin your composition?

_____ a compelling or surprising fact

_____ a thought-provoking question

_____ an interesting quotation

_____ a vivid description of an event

_____ a sentence that states the main idea or topic

_____ an opinion

_____ a statement addressed directly to the reader

_____ other _____

2. What is the main idea of your composition?

_____

_____

_____

_____

_____

3. What are three details that you use to support your main idea?

_____

_____

_____

_____

_____

4. Does your composition have a clear beginning, middle, and end?

Yes _____   No _____

5. Write down three examples of descriptive or interesting details that you used in your composition.

_____

_____

_____

_____

_____

6. What do you want your readers to learn from reading this composition?

_____

_____

_____

_____

_____

7. How do you end your composition?

_____ summarize or restate the main idea

_____ address the reader directly

_____ make a prediction or comment on the future

_____ express an opinion

_____ express a thought, feeling, or statement related to the main idea

_____ leave the reader wondering about an unanswered question

_____ other _____

8. What are three possible titles for your composition?

_____

_____

_____

Pablo's English teacher asks him to write an expository composition in response to this prompt:

> Gambling is illegal in most states. Lottery is a form of gambling. Despite that, playing the lottery is legal in forty of the fifty states. What, exactly, is the lottery? Who benefits from it? How might playing the lottery hurt someone? Why is playing the lottery legal in so many states when other types of gambling such as casinos, horse racing, and sports betting are not? Write a composition that attempts to explain what you think the difference might be between lotteries and other types of gambling. **Without taking a side**, try to get your readers to think more deeply about this conflicting issue.

Here is one of Malcolm's drafts. Read it and then answer the questions that follow.

Malcolm's Draft A

What is the difference between the person who loses a thousand dollars playing blackjack at the casino and the person who spends a thousand dollars on hundreds of losing lottery tickets? NONE! Technically, there is absolutely no difference. Yet, despite the fact that playing the lottery is a form of gambling, it is allowed in many states across the nation. Why? Unfortunately, this controversial question has no clear answer.

Gambling is defined as any behavior involving the risk of money or valuables. As most anyone would acknowledge, gambling is dangerous. People can become addicted to gambling. They might not be able to stop, even after they lose everything that they own. Recognizing this, most states have made all forms of gambling illegal—all forms, that is, except the lottery. A popular form of gambling, the lottery is actually legal in forty out of the fifty states in the union, and, as with most other controversial issues, this one has two clearly opposing sides.

Those against a legalized lottery argue that playing the lottery is addictive, just like other forms of gambling and that, as a result, too many citizens lose their hard-earned money. Even though odds are good that most of these people will lose, they continue to play, day in and day out. This addiction is the danger and the reality of gambling, the opponents say.

On the flip side are the people who believe that the lottery is a harmless game of fun that can actually be beneficial. With so many people playing the lottery, a significant amount of cash accumulates, even after winners are paid off. All that extra money goes to the individual states. It can help pay for education, health, and social service programs. Lottery money can be a terrific resource in the time of a budget crisis or state emergency. The benefits of this extra money cannot be disputed or ignored, supporters insist.

(continued on next page)

64

(continued from previous page)

> Regardless of which position you take on the issue and regardless of how harmless (or not) you think the lottery is, the fact remains that it is a form of gambling. In the end, it's your choice whether or not to pull out your wallet and pick the numbers. So, what's it's going to be—will you play or will you stay?

1. How does the writer begin the composition?

   _____ a compelling or surprising fact

   _____ a thought-provoking question

   _____ an interesting quotation

   _____ a vivid description of an event

   _____ a sentence that states the main idea or topic

   _____ an opinion

   _____ a statement addressed directly to the reader

   _____ other _____

2. What is the main idea of the composition?

   _____

   _____

   _____

   _____

3. What are some details that support the main idea in this composition?

   _____

   _____

   _____

   _____

4. Is this composition well organized and easy to follow?   Yes _____   No _____

5. A good composition has a clear beginning, middle, and end. Number the paragraphs in order as they occur. Tell which numbers are beginning paragraphs, which are middle paragraphs, and which are ending paragraphs.

_____

_____

_____

6. Descriptive details are details that help readers to get good pictures in their minds as they read. Underline five descriptive details in this draft.

7. Is there any information that does not belong in this draft?

_____

_____

_____

8. On a scale from 1 to 10, with 10 being the best, how would you rate this draft? Tell why.

_____

_____

_____

_____

9. How does the writer end the composition?

_____   summarizes or restates the main idea

_____   addresses the reader directly

_____   makes a prediction or comments on the future

_____   expresses an opinion

_____   expresses a thought, feeling, or statement related to the main idea

_____   leaves the reader wondering about an unanswered question

_____   other _____

Here is Pablo's other draft. Read it and then answer the questions that follow.

Pablo's Draft B

Gambling is defined as any behavior involving the risk of money or valuables on the outcome of a game or contest in which the outcome is dependent upon chance. As most anyone would acknowledge, gambling can be very dangerous. People can become addicted to gambling. They might not be able to stop, even after they lose everything they own. It's terrible. Recognizing this, most states have made all forms of gambling illegal. All forms, that is, except the lottery. A popular form of gambling, the lottery is actually legal in forty out of the fifty states in the union.

Since the lottery is legal and much more accessible than other forms of gambling, millions of people every day spend their hard-earned money on playing the lottery. Unfortunately, the only odds in their favor are the odds that they will lose their money. Yet people continue to play this game, and hundreds of thousands of millions of dollars are lost by the citizens of this country every year. Millions of citizens across the nation suffer from serious gambling problems resulting from playing the lottery. Just as in other forms of gambling such as can be found at casinos or horse races, too people go bankrupt in their attempt to hit it big. As a result, opponents believe that if the lottery were made illegal, fewer people would run the risk of losing everything.

I think that they are right. If they would just make lotteries illegal, not as many people would play it. Some people would still play it though, just like people all across the country gamble at casinos or racetracks. Even though they are illegal, they are still pretty much accepted and people still do them. So it's not as if the lottery would go out of business. They would still have plenty of underground business. The only thing that would change is that most of the people who not do it, since they wouldn't want to run the risk of getting caught and in trouble by the law.

In my opinion, there is nothing good that could come from any gambling. People can't help themselves. They lose so much money all the time in casinos, racetracks, sporting pools, and even in the stock market. It's all risky. When people lose their money on stuff like this, they can hit some really hard times. If it wasn't available to people, they wouldn't hit such hard times. It's the same as smoking cigarettes. If cigarettes weren't available, people wouldn't get so many disease related to smoking. Lung cancer is one of the biggest killers of people in this country. A lot of that is due to smoking.

Even if they don't take gambling away totally, they could at least make the lottery illegal so fewer people would play it. That would help tremendously.

10. How does the writer begin the composition?

_____ a compelling or surprising fact

_____ a thought-provoking question

_____ an interesting quotation

_____ a vivid description of an event

_____ a sentence that states the main idea or topic

_____ an opinion

_____ a statement addressed directly to the reader

_____ other _____

11. What is the main idea of the composition?

_____

_____

_____

_____

12. Is this composition well organized and easy to follow?   Yes _____   No _____

13. What are some details that support the main idea in this composition?

_____

_____

_____

_____

14. Descriptive details are details that help readers to get good pictures in their minds as they read. Underline five descriptive details in this draft.

15. A good composition has a clear beginning, middle, and end. Number the paragraphs in order as they occur. Tell which numbers are beginning paragraphs, which are middle paragraphs, and which are ending paragraphs.

_____

_____

_____

16. Is there any information that does not belong in this draft?

_____

_____

_____

17. On a scale from 1 to 10, with 10 being the best, how would you rate this draft? Tell why.

_____

_____

_____

_____

18. How does the writer end the composition?

_____   summarizes or restates the main idea

_____   addresses the reader directly

_____   makes a prediction or comments on the future

_____   expresses an opinion

_____   expresses a thought, feeling, or statement related to the main idea

_____   leaves the reader wondering about an unanswered question

_____   other _____

19. You have now read two drafts of Pablo's work. One is the rough draft, and one is an improved draft.

    Which do you think is the improved draft?   Draft A _____   Draft B _____

20. Tell why you chose this draft.

    _____

    _____

    _____

    _____

    _____

    _____

    _____

21. Sum up the improved draft of this controversial topic in one paragraph, being sure to clearly state what both sides of the issue are.

    _____

    _____

    _____

    _____

    _____

    _____

    _____

    _____

Now it's your turn. *Write an expository composition in response to this prompt and then answer the questions that follow.*

Many schools, churches, and associations in towns and cities across the United States hold raffles to raise money for certain things. In a raffle, people purchase tickets in the hopes of winning a prize. How is this different from playing the lottery? Write a composition telling how raffles do or do not differ from lotteries and other forms of illegal gambling.

AS YOU WRITE YOUR COMPOSITION, REMEMBER TO:

- Begin the composition with a topic sentence.

- Choose at least three details to support your topic sentence.

- End with an idea that restates or pulls together the main topic or idea.

_____

_____

_____

_____

_____

_____

_____

_____

_____

_____

_____

1. How do you begin your composition?

   _____ a compelling or surprising fact

   _____ a thought-provoking question

   _____ an interesting quotation

   _____ a vivid description of an event

   _____ a sentence that states the main idea or topic

   _____ an opinion

   _____ a statement addressed directly to the reader

   _____ other _____

2. What is the main idea of your composition?

   _____

   _____

   _____

   _____

3. What are three details that you use to support your main idea?

   _____

   _____

   _____

   _____

4. Does your composition have a clear beginning, middle, and end?

   Yes _____   No _____

74

5. Write down three examples of descriptive or interesting details that you used in your composition.

_____

_____

_____

_____

_____

6. What do you want your readers to learn from reading this composition?

_____

_____

_____

_____

_____

7. How do you end your composition?

_____ summarize or restate the main idea

_____ address the reader directly

_____ make a prediction or comment on the future

_____ express an opinion

_____ express a thought, feeling, or statement related to the main idea

_____ leave the reader wondering about an unanswered question

_____ other _____

8. What are three possible titles for your composition?

_____

_____

_____

Georgia's English teacher asks her to write an expository composition in response to this prompt:

> What is ESP? Who experiences ESP? What does it feel like? Is it real or imaginary? What are your personal experiences with it?

Here is one of Georgia's drafts. Read it and then answer the questions that follow.

Georgia's Draft A

One time at school, I had ESP about my grandmother. It turned out to be true. In my opinion, it was no coincidence that I had a strange feeling about my grandmother that day. I believe that it was ESP.

There are tons of different types of ESP out there. Telepathy is the ability to read another person's thoughts. Clairvoyance is seeing thing happening somewhere else. Precognition is seeing the future. Retrocognition is the past. Mediumship is the ability to communicate with the dead. Déjà vu is the feeling that you had this happened before. It can all be eerie and really weird, but also fascinating. I have experienced a number of these types of ESP before. Most of us probablyl have. Even if you don't realize it.

What it all means is that you kind of get a sense or a feeling from somewhere. Think about how you see or hear things or smell or taste or touch things. You get information about what's going on around by using your five senses, sight, hearing, touching, smelling and tasting. Well, ESP, it's like another sense—a sixth sense. It's information you get, but not from those five ways, hearing tasting, seeing, touching, etc. It from a different way that you can't quite put your finger on. It's hard to explain.

You might hear about it all the time, like the times when a mother had a feeling that she shouldn't let her child go in a car with someone, so she didn't, but right after that, the person got in a bad car accident and then there are times when someone thinks about an old friend, and suddenly, that old friend calls up out of nowhere. There are times when you feel like you know exactly what is going to happen, and then out of nowhere, it really does. There are times when you feel like you've been in this exact same situation before thats déjà vu. There are times when you think you might have talked to someone who is no longer alive. There are so many different types and instance of ESP that it's hard to describe them all here all at once.

Even if many of us have times once in a while when we think we have some form of this, there are people who are totally on control of their ESP. They claim to have it all the time and they can use it whenever they please. These people are known as fortune tellers, psychics, gypsies, clairvoyants, etc. You have probably seen them in the movies. They actually do this ESP thing as a profession it is how they earn their living they will communicate in the past, the present, and the future—whatever it is that people will

(continued on next page)

(continued from previous page)

pay them to do. Some of these psychics seem to be good. Some have actually helped police officers, detectives, and investigators solve crimes. Others are pretty bad and are only just only looking for a way to make money off the poor people.

Regardless of whether or not the people are real or not, the fact remains that ESP seems to be real because it seems that everybody has had some sort of real situation where they really feel like something strange has taken place and they can't really explain it in any way except ESP, or the sixth sense.

In fact, there have been a few movies done on this subject. Quite a few actually. One movie in fact was called The Sixth Sense, which starred Bruce Willis and Haley Joel Osment. It had to do with the dead being able to communicate with those that are alive. It's kind of fascinating.

Whether or not ESP and the sixth sense is a real phenomenon, we are each entitled to have our own opinions on the subject. I know what mine is. What's yours?

1. How does the writer begin the composition?

_____ a compelling or surprising fact

_____ a thought-provoking question

_____ an interesting quotation

_____ a vivid description of an event

_____ a sentence that states the main idea or topic

_____ an opinion

_____ a statement addressed directly to the reader

_____ other _____

2. What is the main idea of the composition?

_____

_____

_____

_____

3. What are three details that support the main idea in this composition?

_____

_____

_____

_____

4. Is there any information that does not belong in this draft?

_____

_____

_____

_____

5. A good composition has a clear beginning, middle, and end. Number the paragraphs in order as they occur. Tell which numbers are beginning paragraphs, which are middle paragraphs, and which are ending paragraphs.

_____

_____

_____

6. A good writer tries to avoid run-on and incomplete sentences. If there are any examples of run-on or incomplete sentences in this draft, write them here.

_____

_____

_____

_____

_____

7. What is a *phenomenon*?

   a. a child actor
   b. a ghost
   c. a remarkable occurrence
   d. ESP

8. According to the author, what is the *sixth sense*?

   _____

   _____

   _____

   _____

9. How does the writer end the composition?

   _____ summarizes or restates the main idea

   _____ addresses the reader directly

   _____ makes a prediction or comments on the future

   _____ expresses an opinion

   _____ expresses a thought, feeling, or statement related to the main idea

   _____ leaves the reader wondering about an unanswered question

   _____ other _____

Here is Georgia's other draft. Read it and then answer the questions that follow.

Georgia's Draft B

Last year, I was sitting in math class taking a test, when I had a very strong feeling that something was wrong. I couldn't put my finger on exactly what it was, but I felt that it had something to do with my grandmother. After a while, I became far too distracted to focus on the test, so I requested permission to go to the nurse. On my way there, I heard my name paged on the loudspeaker. I was being called to the office. When I got there, my mom was waiting for me. She told me that Grandma had suffered a stroke the previous night and was in the hospital. We left immediately to go and be with her.

In my opinion, it was no coincidence that I had a strange feeling about my grandmother that day. I believe that it was my sixth sense at work. Every day of our

(continued on next page)

(continued from previous page)

lives, we rely on our five senses to help us to hear, smell, taste, see, and touch things. These senses are how we experience the world around us. Without them, we would not know what was going on around us. I think that the sixth sense is just as present in all of us as the other five senses are.

This sixth sense is the one that's most difficult to explain and understand because it can take on so many various forms. Have you ever had a feeling that something was going to happen and it does? Have you ever experienced the strange sensation of knowing something has happened and it has? Have you ever known what someone was thinking? Have you ever simply known something that was just plain impossible to know?

The sixth sense, also known as ESP, or "ExtraSensory Perception," has been the subject of dispute for years. There are many differing opinions in regard to the existence of this phenomenon. Some people believe that every human being has experienced the sixth sense. Others believe that only a small number of psychic individuals like fortunetellers and clairvoyants have this ability. Certain religions teach that this particular sensation is the way in which an omnipotent being communicates with humans. Still others do not believe that it exists at all—that it is a figment of overly-active imaginations.

There are a number of different types of ESP. Telepathy is the ability to read another person's thoughts. Clairvoyance is the ability to see events happening somewhere else. Precognition is the ability to see into the future. Retrocognition is the ability to see into the past. Mediumship is the ability to communicate with the dead. Déjà vu is the feeling that, although you are experiencing something for the first time, you feel as though you have experienced that exact situation before.

While nobody can ever know for sure what the real truth is about this phenomenon, and whether or not these types of ESP actually exist in some form or other, there are plenty of well-documented examples that seem to prove the theory that at least some form of a sixth sense does indeed exist. In addition to stories like my own, there are many professional psychics out there who seem to have been able to prove their abilities. On a few occasions, these psychics have actually assisted detectives in solving mysteries by helping investigators to find missing persons and leading them directly to crime scenes.

Another example of the existence of ESP is the work of Nostradamus. He was a physician and astrologer who lived in the sixteenth century and claimed to foresee events of the future. He published hundreds of his predictions, and it is believed that many of those have indeed come to pass, including the reign of Napoleon, the rise and fall of Adolf Hitler, the first moon landing, the use of the atom bomb, and the assassination of President John F. Kennedy.

Whether or not ESP and the sixth sense is a real phenomenon, we are each entitled to have our own opinions on the subject. I know what mine is. What's yours?

10. What is the main idea of the composition?

_____

_____

_____

_____

11. How does the writer begin the composition?

_____   a compelling or surprising fact

_____   a thought-provoking question

_____   an interesting quotation

_____   a vivid description of an event

_____   a sentence that states the main idea or topic

_____   an opinion

_____   a statement addressed directly to the reader

_____   other _____

12. A good composition has a clear beginning, middle, and end. Number the paragraphs in order as they occur. Tell which numbers are beginning paragraphs, which are middle paragraphs, and which are ending paragraphs.

_____

_____

_____

13. What are three details that support the main idea in this composition?

_____

_____

_____

_____

14. A good writer tries to avoid run-on and incomplete sentences. If there are any examples of run-on or incomplete sentences in this draft, write them here.

_____

_____

_____

_____

15. According to the author, what is *déjà vu*?

_____

_____

_____

_____

16. Is there any information that does not belong in this draft?

_____

_____

_____

17. The following sentence is found in this draft:

> *Certain religions teach that this particular sensation is the way in*
>
> *which an* **omnipotent** *being communicates with humans.*

In this sentence, what does the word *omnipotent* mean?

a. knowing everything
b. imaginary
c. having unlimited power, Godlike
d. gigantic

18. How does the writer end the composition?

     _____   summarizes or restates the main idea

     _____   addresses the reader directly

     _____   makes a prediction or comments on the future

     _____   expresses an opinion

     _____   expresses a thought, feeling, or statement related to the main idea

     _____   leavess the reader wondering about an unanswered question

     _____   other _____

19. You have now read two drafts of Georgia's work. One is her rough draft, and one is an improved draft.

    Which do you think is the improved draft?   Draft A _____   Draft B _____

20. Tell why you chose this draft.

_____

_____

_____

_____

_____

_____

_____

_____

_____

Now it's your turn. Write an expository composition in response to this prompt and then answer the questions that follow.

Is ESP real? What is *your* opinion? Do *you* have personal experiences with ESP in any one of its forms? Do *you* think that ESP should be officially labeled as our sixth sense? Should people take ESP more or less seriously than they currently do? Tell why you believe what you believe about ESP.

AS YOU WRITE YOUR COMPOSITION, REMEMBER TO:

- Begin the composition with a topic sentence.

- Choose at least three details to support your topic sentence.

- End with an idea that restates or pulls together the main topic or idea.

_____

_____

_____

_____

_____

_____

_____

_____

_____

_____

_____

_____

1. How do you begin your composition?

    _____   a compelling or surprising fact

    _____   a thought-provoking question

    _____   an interesting quotation

    _____   a vivid description of an event

    _____   a sentence that states the main idea or topic

    _____   an opinion

    _____   a statement addressed directly to the reader

    _____   other _____

2. What is the main idea of your composition?

    _____

    _____

    _____

    _____

3. What are three details that you use to support your main idea?

    _____

    _____

    _____

    _____

4. Does your composition have a clear beginning, middle, and end?

    Yes _____   No _____

87

5. Write down three examples of descriptive or interesting details that you used in your composition.

    _____

    _____

    _____

    _____

    _____

6. What do you want your readers to learn from reading this composition?

    _____

    _____

    _____

    _____

    _____

7. How do you end your composition?

    _____   summarize or restate the main idea

    _____   address the reader directly

    _____   make a prediction or comment on the future

    _____   express an opinion

    _____   express a thought, feeling, or statement related to the main idea

    _____   leave the reader wondering about an unanswered question

    _____   other _____

8. What are three possible titles for your composition?

    _____

    _____

    _____

Topic 8: Rap in Time

Maria's English teacher asks her to write an expository composition in response to this prompt:

> What is rap music? Where and how did this type of music originate? How is it different from other types of music? How can rap music affect society? In what ways is this type of music beneficial? In what ways could it be considered detrimental? From your own experiences and observations, tell what you know about rap music.

Here is one of Maria's drafts. Read it and then answer the questions that follow.

Maria's Draft A

You better lose yourself in the music, the moment
You own it, you better never let it go
You only got one shot, do not miss your chance to blow
This opportunity comes once in a lifetime, yo

With these inspirational lyrics to the song, "Lose Yourself," Marshall Mathers III (otherwise known as Eminem) won an Oscar for Best Original Song at the 2003 Academy Awards. It was the first rap song to ever receive this widely recognized and prestigious award. Today, artists like Usher, 50 Cent, Nelly, and Kanye West are also seeing their albums explode in popularity as more and more people are being introduced to the rhythmical and oftentimes controversial sounds of rap.

Rap, in some form or another, existed long before these modern-day artists were even born. Storytelling, singing, and verbal jousting were all early forms of rapping, used by Africans Americans for centuries as a means of cultural expression. It gave them a way to express grief and joy, and to celebrate their ancestry.

It wasn't until the late 1960s however, that the sound as we know it today, came into being when a Jamaican-born DJ introduced the practice of improvising rhymes to music into the African-American culture of New York City. The result was a perfectly matched cultural marriage and, consequently, rap was born.

The social impact was immediately evident. Young urban residents of the Bronx, suffering the effects of a culture of crime, poverty, unemployment, depression, and drug use, were able to use rap as the perfect outlet to express their emotions and frustrations. Requiring no money or lessons, having no concrete rules or boundaries, everyone had access to it. Even in its infant stages, rap established itself as a tremendously influential powerhouse.

(continued on next page)

(continued from previous page)

In 1984, Run D.M.C. became the first rap group to break into mainstream society. From there, artists like 2 Live Crew, the Beastie Boys, LL Cool J, and Public Enemy started making enormous strides in increasing the popularity of rap music. It has only continued to grow since then.

However, it's not been an entirely uphill ride for rap and, as much as it's grown in popularity, it's also grown in controversy. Many opponents of rap music, from the beginning, have considered some of it to be vulgar and offensive. Indeed, there is no disputing that some rap lyrics can be filled with profanity and hateful words.

It's a dilemma to be sure. The United States is a country in which freedom of speech is one of our most beloved privileges. Art, including music, gives us an opportunity to express ourselves in this way. However, we are also a nation that has historically struggled with human and equal rights. Should people be allowed to freely express themselves in a way that could be sexist or racist, as some rap lyrics are? Should such potentially hurtful lyrics be banned?

Regardless of the outcome of this ongoing dispute, many rap artists prove each and every day that their music can be popular, successful, groundbreaking, respectful, and enjoyable all at once to a wide and diverse audience. These men and women prove that rap is, indeed, an art, a form of expression that others can appreciate and enjoy.

1. How does the writer begin the composition?

   _____ a compelling or surprising fact

   _____ a thought-provoking question

   _____ an interesting quotation

   _____ a vivid description of an event

   _____ a sentence that states the main idea or topic

   _____ an opinion

   _____ a statement addressed directly to the reader

   _____ other _____

2. What is the main idea of the composition?

   _____

   _____

   _____

   _____

3.   What are some details that support the main idea in this composition?

_____

_____

_____

_____

4.   Is this composition well organized and easy to follow?   Yes _____   No _____

5.   Descriptive details are details that help readers to get good pictures in their minds as they read. Underline five descriptive details in this draft.

6.   Draw a line through any information that does not belong in this draft.

7.   On a scale from 1 to 10, with 10 being the best, how would you rate the introduction of this draft? Tell why.

_____

_____

_____

_____

8.   A good composition has a clear beginning, middle, and end. Number the paragraphs in order as they occur. Tell which numbers are beginning paragraphs, which are middle paragraphs, and which are ending paragraphs.

_____

_____

_____

9. How does the writer end the composition?

_____ summarizes or restates the main idea

_____ addresses the reader directly

_____ makes a prediction or comments on the future

_____ expresses an opinion

_____ expresses a thought, feeling, or statement related to the main idea

_____ leaves the reader wondering about an unanswered question

_____ other _____

Here is Maria's other draft. Read it and then answer the questions that follow.

Maria's Draft B

Its roots are embedded deep in African-American and Jamaican cultures. Early forms were storytelling, singing, verbal jousting, and other oral similar traditions. It was used as a means of cultural expression and remembers the ancestors. Do you think that anyone way back then ever thought that it would become what is today?

However, it's not been an entirely uphill ride. It's grown in popularity but it has also grown in controversy. Many opponents of it, from the beginning, have considered some of it to be vulgar and offensive. Indeed, there is no disputing that some of the lyrics can be filled with profanity and hateful words. Some people also complain that movies, television, shows, radio shows, magazines, and other things can be vulgar and offensive too with the kinds of stuff that the have nowadays.

Back in the beginning, however, it had an immediate social impact. It gave young urban residents of the Bronx in New York City, who were suffering the effects of a culture of crime, poverty, unemployment, depression, and drug use, the perfect outlet to express their emotions and frustrations. Required no money or lessons, had no concrete rules or boundaries, everyone had access to it. Even in its infant stages, it was becoming really popular really fast. It was just the perfect thing at the perfect time, like the saying being in the right place at the right time.

In 1984, Run D.M.C. became the first group to break into the mainstream. From there, artists like 2 Live Crew, the Beastie Boys, LL Cool J, and Public Enemy started making enormous strides in increasing its popularity. It has only continued to grow since then. Today, artists like Usher, 50 Cent, Nelly, Kanye West, Ludacris, 2pac, Snoop Dog, and L'il Kim are seeing their albums get more popular and famous as more and more people are liking the rhythmical, lively sounds.

It was in the late 1960s, however, that the sound of it as we know it today, was born. A Jamaican-born DJ called Kool Herc, introduced the Jamaican method of "toasting" into the African American culture of the Bronx in New York City. "Toasting",

(continued on next page)

(continued from previous page)

the act of improvising rhymes to music, was a perfectly suited match for African American culture and the result was the creation of a new sound: rap.

Look how far it's come. Marshall Mathers III (otherwise known as Eminem) won an Oscar for Best Original Song at the 2003 Academy Awards. It was the first rap song to ever receive this award ever. It's all a dilemma though. The United States is a free country in which freedom of speech is one of our most beloved privileges. Art, including music, gives us an opportunity to express ourselves in this way. Other forms of art include painting, drawing, sculpting, writing, and others. There are so many ways to express yourself.

10. How does the writer begin the composition?

_____ a compelling or surprising fact

_____ a thought-provoking question

_____ an interesting quotation

_____ a vivid description of an event

_____ a sentence that states the main idea or topic

_____ an opinion

_____ a statement addressed directly to the reader

_____ other _____

11. What is the main idea of the composition?

_____

_____

_____

_____

12. Descriptive details are details that help readers to get good pictures in their minds as they read. Underline five descriptive details in this draft.

13. Draw a line through any information that does not belong in this draft.

14. What are some details that support the main idea in this composition?

_____

_____

_____

_____

15. On a scale from 1 to 10, with 10 being the best, how would you rate the introduction of this draft?

_____

_____

_____

_____

16. A good composition has a clear beginning, middle, and end. Number the paragraphs in order as they occur. Tell which numbers are beginning paragraphs, which are middle paragraphs, and which are ending paragraphs.

_____

_____

_____

17. Is this composition well organized and easy to follow?   Yes _____   No _____

18. How does the writer end the composition?

_____   summarizes or restates the main idea

_____   addresses the reader directly

_____   makes a prediction or comments on the future

_____   expresses an opinion

_____   expresses a thought, feeling, or statement related to the main idea

_____   leaves the reader wondering about an unanswered question

_____   other _____

19. You have now read two drafts of Maria's work. One is the rough draft, and one is an improved draft.

Which do you think is the improved draft?   Draft A _____   Draft B _____

20. Tell why you chose this draft.

_____

_____

_____

_____

_____

_____

_____

21. Rewrite and improve the following sentence:

It came from the resulting of a combination from the marrying of

African, American, and Jamaican cultures.

_____

_____

_____

_____

95

Now it's your turn. Write an expository composition in response to this prompt and then answer the questions that follow.

> Why are so many kids and adults drawn to music? What is it about music that people love so passionately? Why do different types of music (rap, emo, classical, rock, country) appeal to different people? Tell what you know about music from your personal experience.

AS YOU WRITE YOUR COMPOSITION, REMEMBER TO:

- Begin the composition with a topic sentence.

- Choose at least three details to support your topic sentence.

- End with an idea that restates or pulls together the main topic or idea.

_____

_____

_____

_____

_____

_____

_____

_____

_____

_____

_____

_____

_____

_____

1. How do you begin your composition?

    _____ a compelling or surprising fact

    _____ a thought-provoking question

    _____ an interesting quotation

    _____ a vivid description of an event

    _____ a sentence that states the main idea or topic

    _____ an opinion

    _____ a statement addressed directly to the reader

    _____ other _____

2. What is the main idea of your composition?

    _____

    _____

    _____

    _____

3. What are three details that you use to support your main idea?

    _____

    _____

    _____

    _____

4. Does your composition have a clear beginning, middle, and end?

    Yes _____   No _____

5. Write down three examples of descriptive or interesting details that you used in your composition.

_____

_____

_____

_____

_____

6. What do you want your readers to learn from reading this composition?

_____

_____

_____

_____

7. How do you end your composition?

_____   summarize or restate the main idea

_____   address the reader directly

_____   make a prediction or comment on the future

_____   express an opinion

_____   express a thought, feeling, or statement related to the main idea

_____   leave the reader wondering about an unanswered question

_____   other _____

8. What are three possible titles for your composition?

_____

_____

_____

Topic 9: Integrity

Dennis's English teacher asks him to write an expository composition in response to this prompt:

> What is integrity? What are some of the traits affiliated with integrity? What are some of its opposite traits? Why is integrity important? What can happen when integrity is lacking? Who are some people of integrity? Who are some people who lack integrity?

Here is one of Dennis's drafts. Read it and then answer the questions that follow.

Dennis's Draft A

If you discovered a wallet filled with money and an extensive selection of credit cards, what would you do? If you badly damaged an antique lamp, but your mom thought that your little brother did it, would you say something? If the new kid in school were being taunted and bullied by all your best friends, would you intervene? If your teacher inadvertently left the answers to the final exam out where you could see them, would you look? If you had to take a stand for something that you strongly believe in, but nobody supported you, how would that make you feel?

Are you a person of integrity? Take the following quiz to find out.
Remember, be honest and true to yourself when you answer the questions.

1. I always try to do what is right, even when it's tough.   Yes ____ No ____
2. I don't give in to pressure and temptation.   Yes ____ No ____
3. I try to be the very best person I can be.   Yes ____ No ____
4. People can trust me to always tell the truth.   Yes ____ No ____

If you answered, "Yes," to these four questions, you are most likely a person of integrity. Integrity is a character trait in which you have the inner strength to be truthful, trustworthy, good, and honest in all things, at all times. It means you act justly and honorably. It means you have strong moral principles and personal values. It means you have respect for all people and all things.

Despite the fact that it may sound easy to be a person of integrity, so many people nowadays are not. On the contrary, many people in this day and age are deceitful, corrupt, dishonest, and immoral. Just turn on the six o'clock news this evening. This ever-increasing lack of integrity seems to know no bounds. It exists everywhere from the poorest streets of our most dangerous cities to multi-million dollar luxurious mansions in the suburbs, from the basketball courts of the NBA to the White House. It has become prevalent in our businesses, prisons, police departments, and even in our schools. There is crime, deception, dishonor, and cruelty everywhere you look.

(continued on next page)

101

(continued from previous page)

So, in this day and age when corruption, disrespect, and dishonesty have become so rampant and out of control, can integrity possibly matter anymore? Do you believe that having and displaying integrity can actually make a difference?

I do. I believe that, like a chain reaction, a person who does the right thing will inspire other people to do the right thing. I think that it is easier for people to make the right choices in their lives when they see others making the right choices in theirs.

So how can we start a chain reaction of integrity? It's really quite simple. Most of us already know right from wrong. So, once we are presented with a situation where we must make some sort of decision as to how to behave or respond, we must make the right choice, no matter how hard it is, no matter what kind of pressure we are experiencing to do the opposite. That determination to do right, and that alone, will start to make an impact. If each and every one of us makes the effort to do this without fail, we will undoubtedly witness a significant change taking place inside. If each and every one of us teaches and encourages the people around us to behave in accordance with this ideal, the change will become expansive and will find its way to all corners of society.

How do you want people to remember you when you're gone? Do you want them to remember you as a liar and a cheat—someone nobody could ever trust or respect? Or, on the other hand, do you want to be remembered as a person of integrity, good judgment, and sound character? It's your choice. It's your life. How you choose to live it is up to you. Which path are you going to take?

1. How does the writer begin the composition?

_____ a compelling or surprising fact

_____ a thought-provoking question

_____ an interesting quotation

_____ a vivid description of an event

_____ a sentence that states the main idea or topic

_____ an opinion

_____ a statement addressed directly to the reader

_____ other _____

2. What is the main idea of the composition?

_____

_____

_____

3. What are three details that support the main idea in this composition?

_____

_____

_____

4. A good composition has a clear beginning, middle, and end. Number the paragraphs in order as they occur. Tell which numbers are beginning paragraphs, which are middle paragraphs, and which are ending paragraphs.

_____

_____

_____

5. What is *integrity*?

   a. good character
   b. intelligence
   c. creativity
   d. immorality

6. Is there any information that does not belong in this draft?

_____

_____

_____

7. Was the writer's use of the questions and the quiz at the beginning of the composition effective in sparking your interest as a reader?   Yes _____   No _____

    Tell why or why not.

    _____

    _____

    _____

    _____

8. What are three things you learned in this composition that you didn't already know?

    _____

    _____

    _____

    _____

9. How does the writer end the composition?

    _____   summarizes or restates the main idea

    _____   addresses the reader directly

    _____   makes a prediction or comments on the future

    _____   expresses an opinion

    _____   expresses a thought, feeling, or statement related to the main idea

    _____   leaves the reader wondering about an unanswered question

    _____   other _____

Here is Dennis's other draft. Read it and then answer the questions that follow.

Dennis's Draft B

There's simply not a lot of it in this day and age. It's too bad because it is a fantastic characteristic to have. If you don't have it, you should get some. It's too bad they don't sell it in the local pharmacy, because that would be much easier. You're doctor would just have to prescribe it for you and you would take a pill and have some just like that! Unfortunately, it's just not that easy. It's just not how it used to be.

(continued on next page)

(continued from previous page)

In the olden days, people really had a lot of integrity. It was just a way of life. It was just expected of everybody. That's just the way it was. Parents taught their kids all about the proper way to behave and to act in all sort of situations. They taught their kids to have dignity and respect for others. They taught their kids to do the right thing in any situation, no matter how hard it is.

Nowadays, it seems like even the parents are not doing the right things. So how can they be expected to teach their kids, or model for their kids the kinds of behaviors that include acting with good integrity? It's just impossible and a little bit sad too. How are kids supposed to learn?

Well, there is a saying that goes, "It takes a village…" and what that means is it can take a whole village, or family, or town, or city, or group of people to raise a child. It means that everyone has got to teach that child all about life and how to act, and how to behave and everybody is responsible for helping that child to grow up into a good, strong, adult who has good character. If nobody helps the child to learn these things than how is the child supposed to ever know? Kids aren't just born knowing things like that. We have to teach them. That's why they are kids and adults are adults.

Integrity has a lot of synonyms and they are: honesty, uprightness, moral soundness, principle, character, virtue, purity, decency, self-respect, morality, straight-forwardness, etc. These are directly from the thesaurus so I know they are accurate. We probably all know people who have these traits, and we probably all know people who don't have these traits. There are lot of people lacking in integrity that we read about in the newspapers and see on television. There are a lot of shows on tv. There are a lot of antonyms for the words too.

The only thing we can really do to help to improve the situation is to try to be good people with integrity ourselves and maybe over time, when other people see us doing this, other people will start to do it too. It could be like it were contagious. Usually contagious things are bad, but this could be a good contagion. It's not a bad idea, but everybody would really have to make the effort to do it so that some good would come of it all. I think that is definitely possible to do these things. We just have to focus and concentrate and encourage each other and do it.

10. How does the writer begin the composition?

_____ a compelling or surprising fact

_____ a thought-provoking question

_____ an interesting quotation

_____ a vivid description of an event

_____ a sentence that states the main idea or topic

_____ an opinion

_____ a statement addressed directly to the reader

_____ other _____

11. What is the main idea of the composition?

_____

_____

_____

_____

12. What are three details that support the main idea in this composition?

_____

_____

_____

_____

13. A good composition has a clear beginning, middle, and end. Number the paragraphs in order as they occur. Tell which numbers are beginning paragraphs, which are middle paragraphs, and which are ending paragraphs.

_____

_____

_____

14. Is there any information that does not belong in this draft?

_____

_____

_____

_____

15. Name another word for integrity.

_____

_____

_____

16. Was the writer's introduction effective in sparking your interest as a reader?

    Yes _____   No _____   Tell why or why not.

_____

_____

_____

17. What are three things you learned in this composition that you didn't already know?

_____

_____

_____

_____

18. How does the writer end the composition?

    _____   summarizes or restates the main idea

    _____   addresses the reader directly

    _____   makes a prediction or comments on the future

    _____   expresses an opinion

    _____   expresses a thought, feeling, or statement related to the main idea

    _____   leaves the reader wondering about an unanswered question

    _____   other _____

107

19. You have now read two drafts of Dennis's work. One is his rough draft, and one is an improved draft.

Which do you think is the improved draft?   Draft A _____   Draft B _____

20. Tell why you chose this draft.

_____

_____

_____

_____

_____

_____

21. Rewrite and improve the following sentence:

Haveing integritty means haveing good morale caracter, always doing the rite thing, and being somebody somebody can trust.

_____

_____

_____

_____

Now it's your turn. Write an expository composition in response to this prompt and then answer the questions that follow.

> What beliefs are most important to you? Why are they so important? From whom did you learn them? What are some examples of how you try to live by those beliefs? How do you stand up for these beliefs when others go against them?

AS YOU WRITE YOUR COMPOSITION, REMEMBER TO:

- Begin the composition with a topic sentence.

- Choose at least three details to support your topic sentence.

- End with an idea that restates or pulls together the main topic or idea.

_____

_____

_____

_____

_____

_____

_____

_____

_____

_____

_____

_____

_____

_____

111

1. How do you begin your composition?

    _____   a compelling or surprising fact

    _____   a thought-provoking question

    _____   an interesting quotation

    _____   a vivid description of an event

    _____   a sentence that states the main idea or topic

    _____   an opinion

    _____   a statement addressed directly to the reader

    _____   other _____

2. What is the main idea of your composition?

    _____

    _____

    _____

    _____

    _____

3. What are three details that you use to support your main idea?

    _____

    _____

    _____

    _____

    _____

4. Does your composition have a clear beginning, middle, and end?

    Yes _____   No _____

112

5. Write down three examples of descriptive or interesting details that you used in your composition.

_____

_____

_____

_____

_____

6. What do you want your readers to learn from reading this composition?

_____

_____

_____

_____

_____

7. How do you end your composition?

_____ summarize or restate the main idea

_____ address the reader directly

_____ make a prediction or comment on the future

_____ express an opinion

_____ express a thought, feeling, or statement related to the main idea

_____ leave the reader wondering about an unanswered question

_____ other _____

8. What are three possible titles for your composition?

_____

_____

_____

Topic 10:   Changing Times

Hanna's English teacher asks her to write an expository composition in response to this prompt:

> What is Daylight Saving Time? Why do we have it? When and how did it start? Who uses it? How does it affect us? Why is it controversial? Give your readers an interesting and informational history of Daylight Saving Time.

Here is one of Hanna's drafts. Read it and then answer the questions that follow.

Hanna's Draft A

When World War I began, people saw the benefit of saving daylight. The extension of daylight hours, at least in wartime, helped to conserve fuel and electricity that could be hard to come by during a war. Actually, it's hard to come by in other instances as well, such as when there are oil embargos or shortages or oil tanker crashes. There are different types of fuel and we are fairly reliant upon them all. Anyway, one country after another entered into daylight saving mode during this first war. The United States was no exception and, in 1918, a wartime daylight saving law was passed here. When the war ended, however, the idea of continuing with the time change got unpopular. Most people back then, especially farmers, went to bed and got up early. Without a war, why have it? The law was repealed and only the states of Massachusetts and Rhode Island chose to keep it.

After reverting to daylight saving one more time during the Second World War, the United States left it up to individual states to decide whether or not they wanted a permanent time change. Many did and by 1966, more than one hundred million Americans, as well as travel and broadcasting industries were regularly changing their clocks twice yearly so therefore, The Uniform Time Act of 1966 officially establishing Daylight Saving Time as beginning on the last Sunday in April and ending on the last Sunday in October. States that didn't want to participate did not have to. Hawaii and Arizona (except for Navajo Indian Reservations) chose not to have a time change. Also, the part of the state of Indiana that is one Eastern Standard Time does not either. In 1986, once last change was made: Daylight Saving Time would begin on the first Sunday of April rather than the last and it's remained that way ever since.

1907, however, was when it all really started. A British man who worked as a builder who was named William Willit, who had an interesting idea on his way to work early one spring morning when he observed that even though the sun was out and brightly shining, shades and blinds and curtains were drawn in every home he passed, a telltale sign that its residents were still asleep. He felt that he was witnessing a terrible wasteful use of daylight and as a result, wrote an essay entitled just

(continued on next page)

(continued from previous page)

that—Waste of Daylight. In this essay, he proposed that time be changed as a way get people to start making better use of the daylight. The British government liked his idea and, in 1917, it enacted "British Summer Time."

Daylight Saving Time is considered an issue people do not all agree upon. This is a controversial issue, an issue that people take different sides about. Supporters of Daylight Saving Time say that it conserves energy. They also say too, that fewer accidents and crimes occur when there is daylight. Those people that are against it, on the other hand, argue that this is not true. They say that no significant energy is conserved. They say that more people are involved in accidents and crimes as a resulting from being disoriented from the time changes, kind of like being jet lagged like if you travel by plane to somewhere far away. These opponents hope that one day, the law will not continue.

1. How does the writer begin the composition?

    _____   a compelling or surprising fact

    _____   a thought-provoking question

    _____   an interesting quotation

    _____   a vivid description of an event

    _____   a sentence that states the main idea or topic

    _____   an opinion

    _____   a statement addressed directly to the reader

    _____   other _____

2. What is the main idea of the composition?

    _____

    _____

    _____

    _____

3. Is this composition well organized and easy to follow?   Yes _____   No _____

4. Draw a line through any information that is redundant and/or unnecessary.

5. What are some details that support the main idea in this composition?

_____

_____

_____

_____

6. On a scale from 1 to 10, with 10 being the best, how would you rate the introduction of this draft? Tell why.

_____

_____

_____

_____

7. A good composition has a clear beginning, middle, and end. Number the paragraphs in order as they occur. Tell which numbers are beginning paragraphs, which are middle paragraphs, and which are ending paragraphs.

_____

_____

_____

8. A good composition has varied sentence length. Give one example of a shorter sentence and one example of a longer sentence.

_____

_____

_____

_____

_____

9. How does the writer end the composition?

_____ summarizes or restates the main idea

_____ addresses the reader directly

_____ makes a prediction or comments on the future

_____ expresses an opinion

_____ expresses a thought, feeling, or statement related to the main idea

_____ leaves the reader wondering about an unanswered question

_____ other _____

Here is Hanna's other draft. Read it and then answer the questions that follow.

Hanna's Draft B

Every spring we turn our clocks ahead one hour. Every autumn, we turn them back. Have you ever stopped to think about why we do this?

Daylight Saving Time (not Daylight Savings Time, as many people mistakenly refer to it) is a creative way for humans to make better use of daylight hours. To understand why Daylight Saving Time was created in the first place, we need to go back in time (no pun intended!).

In 1907, almost a hundred years ago, a British builder named William Willit had an interesting idea. On his way to work early one spring morning, he observed that, even though the sun was out and brightly shining, shades and curtains were drawn in every home he passed. This was a telltale sign that the people inside were still asleep. Willit thought that this was a terrible waste of precious daylight. As a result, he wrote an essay entitled just that—"Waste of Daylight." In this essay, he proposed that time be changed as a way to get people to start making better use of the daylight. The British government liked his idea and, in 1917, enacted "British Summer Time," the first official attempt at daylight saving.

When World War I began shortly thereafter, people everywhere immediately saw the benefit of such an idea. The extension of daylight hours, at least in wartime, helped to conserve expensive fuel and electricity. One country after another entered into daylight saving mode. The United States was no exception and, in 1918, a wartime daylight saving law was passed. When the war ended, however, the idea of continuing with the time change quickly became unpopular. Most people back then, especially farmers, went to bed early in the evening and rose early in the morning. Without a war, there seemed to be no valid need for a change. The law was repealed.

After reverting to daylight saving one more time during the Second World War, the United States government left it up to individual states to decide whether or not they wanted to implement a permanent time change. Many did. By 1966, more than one

(continued on next page)

(continued from previous page)

hundred million Americans, as well as the travel and broadcasting industries, were regularly changing their clocks twice yearly. Recognizing this, The Uniform Time Act of 1966 was passed, officially establishing Daylight Saving Time as beginning on the last Sunday in April and ending on the last Sunday in October. States that didn't want to participate did not have to. Hawaii and Arizona (except for Navajo Indian Reservations) chose not to have a time change, as did the eastern part of the state of Indiana. In 1986, one last change was made: Daylight Saving Time would begin on the first Sunday of April rather than the last. It has remained that way ever since.

Despite the fact that the time change seems as though it's finally here to stay, it is still considered a bit of a controversial issue. Supporters of Daylight Saving Time say that, in addition to the conservation of energy, fewer accidents and crimes actually occur during daylight hours. Those against it, on the other hand, argue that this is not true. They say that, on the contrary, no significant amount of energy is conserved and that more people are involved in accidents and crimes as a result of the disorientation caused by time changes. These opponents hope that, one day, the law will be repealed.

So do we continue to spring ahead and fall back or do we leave the clocks alone? In the end, only time will tell.

10. How does the writer begin the composition?

_____ a compelling or surprising fact

_____ a thought-provoking question

_____ an interesting quotation

_____ a vivid description of an event

_____ a sentence that states the main idea or topic

_____ an opinion

_____ a statement addressed directly to the reader

_____ other _____

11. What is the main idea of the composition?

_____

_____

_____

_____

12. Is this composition well organized and easy to follow?   Yes _____   No _____

13. What are some details that support the main idea in this composition?

_____

_____

_____

_____

14. On a scale from 1 to 10, with 10 being the best, how would you rate the introduction of this draft? Tell why.

_____

_____

_____

15. Draw a line through any information that is redundant and/or unnecessary.

16. A good composition has a clear beginning, middle, and end. Number the paragraphs in order as they occur. Tell which numbers are beginning paragraphs, which are middle paragraphs, and which are ending paragraphs.

_____

_____

_____

17. A good composition has varied sentence length. Give one example of a shorter sentence and one example of a longer sentence.

_____

_____

_____

_____

18. How does the writer end the composition?

_____ summarizes or restates the main idea

_____ addresses the reader directly

_____ makes a prediction or comments on the future

_____ expresses an opinion

_____ expresses a thought, feeling, or statement related to the main idea

_____ leaves the reader wondering about an unanswered question

_____ other _____

19. You have now read two drafts of Hanna's work. One is her rough draft, and one is an improved draft.

Which do you think is the improved draft?   Draft A _____   Draft B _____

20. Tell why you chose this draft.

_____

_____

_____

_____

_____

_____

21. Write another possible attention-grabbing introduction for the improved draft.

_____

_____

_____

_____

_____

_____

120

Now it's your turn. Write an expository composition in response to this prompt and then answer the questions that follow.

> We have a number of different time zones in the United States. What are they? Where are they? Why do you think we have them? Why isn't everyone just on the same time? What do you think is the importance of having different time zones in this country? Write an informational composition about time zones.

AS YOU WRITE YOUR COMPOSITION, REMEMBER TO:

- Begin the composition with a topic sentence.

- Choose at least three details to support your topic sentence.

- End with an idea that restates or pulls together the main topic or idea.

_____

_____

_____

_____

_____

_____

_____

_____

_____

_____

_____

_____

_____

1. How do you begin your composition?

   _____ a compelling or surprising fact

   _____ a thought-provoking question

   _____ an interesting quotation

   _____ a vivid description of an event

   _____ a sentence that states the main idea or topic

   _____ an opinion

   _____ a statement addressed directly to the reader

   _____ other _____

2. What is the main idea of your composition?

   _____

   _____

   _____

   _____

   _____

3. What are three details that you use to support your main idea?

   _____

   _____

   _____

   _____

4. Does your composition have a clear beginning, middle, and end?

   Yes _____   No _____

124

5. Write down three examples of descriptive or interesting details that you used in your composition.

    _____

    _____

    _____

    _____

    _____

6. What do you want your readers to learn from reading this composition?

    _____

    _____

    _____

    _____

    _____

7. How do you end your composition?

    _____   summarize or restate the main idea

    _____   address the reader directly

    _____   make a prediction or comment on the future

    _____   express an opinion

    _____   express a thought, feeling, or statement related to the main idea

    _____   leave the reader wondering about an unanswered question

    _____   other _____

8. What are three possible titles for your composition?

    _____

    _____

    _____

Topic 11: Bystanding

Natasha's English teacher asks her to write an expository composition in response to this prompt:

> The "Bystander Effect" is a psychological phenomenon which happens when regular people like you and me do nothing to assist a victim during a crime or an emergency. Have you ever heard about or witnessed the "Bystander Effect"? Have you ever been guilty of it yourself? Tell about any experiences you know regarding this phenomenon and then tell what is being done or what you think should be done in order to combat this problem.

Here is one of Natasha's drafts. Read it and then answer the questions that follow.

Natasha's Draft A

Consider the following true story: Early one morning in 1964, a young woman named Kitty Genovese was returning from her job as the manager of a New York City bar. At 3:45 a.m., she left work, drove home, and had just gotten out of her car when a man approached her. Kitty walked away from him, but he caught up with her and attacked her with a knife. Neighbors, awakened by her screams, peeked out from behind their curtains, but nobody did anything. Kitty tried to drag herself to safety, all the while crying out for help. The attacker, who had run away at first when Kitty started to call for help, returned when he realized that nobody was coming to her aid. He stabbed her again, this time fatally. Police who investigated this crime discovered that thirty-eight people had either seen or heard something during the attack. Unbelievably, not one of them did anything to help.

Most of us have probably seen an example of this "Bystander Effect" occur at one time or another. I personally witnessed this phenomenon a few years ago. It was Thanksgiving Day and my family was late for dinner at my aunt's house. On the highway, we passed a lady whose car had a flat tire. She was holding twin babies and they were both crying and it looked like the lady was about to cry, too. Even though we could tell that she needed help, we figured that somebody else would help her. Dad said that we shouldn't even bother calling the police because everybody nowadays had cell phones and they were probably getting bombarded with calls already. We just went on ahead to dinner.

On our way home three hours later, the lady was still there. This time we stopped. She told my parents that, in all that time, nobody had stopped to help her. We had wrongly assumed that somebody else would come to her rescue. Unfortunately, if everybody makes that assumption, the victim is no better off than he or she was before, as in the case of that nice young mother.

(continued on next page)

Experts believe that there are various reasons why people may do nothing to intervene in the face of a crisis. They say that, when there are a lot of bystanders, everybody tends to assume that somebody else will do something to help. Another reason is that bystanders are frightened or unsure about whether or not they should involve themselves in a potentially dangerous situation. Understandably, they do not want to make things worse or get hurt themselves. Oftentimes, bystanders simply choose not to step in simply because they do not want to get involved with somebody else's problem. Lastly, bystanders don't always realize that something terrible is going on in the first place. Therefore, they see no reason to offer help.

Nowadays, significant changes have been made so that people will not become victims of the "Bystander Effect." For example, neighborhood watches are now commonplace. These are citizen organizations that help to prevent crime and vandalism. Neighbors are encouraged to keep an eye out for any sign of wrongdoing and to contact the local authorities immediately. Another change has been the creation of the Good Samaritan Law. Otherwise known as the Duty to Assist Law, it is a law that states that any person who witnesses some sort of an emergency must assist the person or people involved. Assistance can come in the form of direct intervention, or it can simply mean calling for help. Failure to obey this law can get you in trouble.

So the next time you are around when something bad seems to be happening to someone, and you don't see any action being taken to help that person, do something. Not only will it help the person in need, it's the law!

1. How does the writer begin the composition?

   _____   a compelling or surprising fact

   _____   a thought-provoking question

   _____   an interesting quotation

   _____   a vivid description of an event

   _____   a sentence that states the main idea or topic

   _____   an opinion

   _____   a statement addressed directly to the reader

   _____   other _____

2. What is the main idea of the composition?

_____

_____

_____

_____

3. What are three details that support the main idea in this composition?

_____

_____

_____

_____

4. Is there any information that does not belong in this draft?

_____

_____

_____

5. A good composition has a clear beginning, middle, and end. Number the paragraphs in order as they occur. Tell which numbers are beginning paragraphs, which are middle paragraphs, and which are ending paragraphs.

_____

_____

_____

6. What are three things that you learned in this composition that didn't already know?

_____

_____

_____

7. How do the two scenarios provided by the writer help readers to understand the "Bystander Effect"?

_____

_____

_____

_____

8. How does the writer end the composition?

_____ summarizes or restates the main idea

_____ addresses the reader directly

_____ makes a prediction or comments on the future

_____ expresses an opinion

_____ expresses a thought, feeling, or statement related to the main idea

_____ leaves the reader wondering about an unanswered question

_____ other _____

Here is Natasha's other draft. Read it and then answer the questions that follow.

Natasha's Draft B

This "Bystander Effect" is a psychological phenomenon in which regular people like you and me do absolutely nothing to help somebody else out of they are being a victim during a crime or an emergency or if they just need some help. I think that it is definitely not a good thing.

Experts believe that there are various reasons why people may do nothing to intervene in the face of a crisis. They say that when there are a lot people, everybody really thinks that somebody else will do it. Another reason is that bystanders are frightened or unsure whether or not they should involve themselves in a potentially dangerous situation because they do not want to make it more worse. Bystanders simply choose not to step in simply because they do not want to get involved with somebody elses problem. And bystanders don't always realize that something terrible is going on in the first place therefore they see no reason to offer their help.

The only example here that is maybe excusable is the last one. Those people would be forgiven because they truly don't believe something serious is going on. However, the others really probably should be doing something. That is why many state governments

(continued on next page)

(continued from previous page)

have made laws about this. In many places, it is now illegal not to do anything during an emergency or during a crime. This puts the responsibility on the people who are standing by (the bystanders) while something is happening.In general, it seems that people are doing a lot more nowadays to help each other than they did in the past. Here are two examples from that past and maybe this is why it all came to be known as a phenomenon way back when.

In 1964, a young woman named Kitty Genovese was returning from her job as the manager of a New York City bar. At 3:45 a.m., she left work, drove home, and had just gotten out of her car when a man approached her. Kitty walked away from him, but he caught up with her and attacked her with a knife. Neighbors, awakened by her screams, peaked out from behind their curtains, but nobody did anything. Kitty tried to drag herself to safety, all the while crying out for help. The attacker, who had run away at first when Kitty started to call for help, returned when he realized nobody was coming to her aid. He stabbed her again, this time fatally. Police who investigated this crime discovered that thirty-eight people had either seen or heard something during the attack. Unbelievably, not one of them did anything to help.

Here is the other example. In Detroit in 1995, a young woman named Deletha Ward was driving over a bridge when accidentally she hit another car. When she pulled over to talk to the other driver, he and his passengers got out of their car and began to beat her. Eventually, in a desperate attempt to get away from her them, Deletha jumped from the bridge. And she died. There is a lot of crime in the world today and a lot especially in the United States of America. Sociologists try to figure out why there is a lot of crime. That is what they do.

9. How does the writer begin the composition?

_____ a compelling or surprising fact

_____ a thought-provoking question

_____ an interesting quotation

_____ a vivid description of an event

_____ a sentence that states the main idea or topic

_____ an opinion

_____ a statement addressed directly to the reader

_____ other _____

10. What is the main idea of the composition?

_____

_____

_____

_____

11. What are three details that support the main idea in this composition?

_____

_____

_____

_____

12. A good composition has a clear beginning, middle, and end. Number the paragraphs in order as they occur. Tell which numbers are beginning paragraphs, which are middle paragraphs, and which are ending paragraphs.

_____

_____

_____

13. Is there any information that does not belong in this draft?

_____

_____

_____

_____

131

14. What are three things that you learned in this composition that didn't already know?

15. What are some reasons the writer gives to explain why bystanders might not do anything in the face of a crisis?

16. How does the writer end the composition?

_____ summarizes or restates the main idea

_____ addresses the reader directly

_____ makes a prediction or comments on the future

_____ expresses an opinion

_____ expresses a thought, feeling, or statement related to the main idea

_____ leaves the reader wondering about an unanswered question

_____ other _____

17. You have now read two drafts of Natasha's work. One is her rough draft, and one is an improved draft.

Which do you think is the improved draft?   Draft A _____   Draft B _____

132

18. Tell why you chose this draft.

_____

_____

_____

_____

_____

_____

_____

_____

19. Rewrite and improve the following sentence:

The bystanding effect is a phenonmenal happening that means its where people just stand there and don't do anything when an ER is going on.

_____

_____

_____

_____

_____

133

Now it's your turn. Write an expository composition in response to this prompt and then answer the questions that follow.

> There are some weird and wacky laws in this country. For example, in New Jersey, it is illegal to slurp soup. In Vermont, every citizen must bathe at least one time per week. In Indiana, on the other hand, it is illegal to bathe during the winter. In Washington, lollipops are illegal. In Florida, housewives can break no more than three dishes per day.
>
> What is a law? Why are laws important in our society? Why is it necessary to abide by the law? Is it ever okay to break the law? Write a composition telling about whether or not it is important to follow laws in the United States.

AS YOU WRITE YOUR COMPOSITION, REMEMBER TO:

- Begin the composition with a topic sentence.

- Choose at least three details to support your topic sentence.

- End with an idea that restates or pulls together the main topic or idea.

1. How do you begin your composition?

    _____ a compelling or surprising fact

    _____ a thought-provoking question

    _____ an interesting quotation

    _____ a vivid description of an event

    _____ a sentence that states the main idea or topic

    _____ an opinion

    _____ a statement addressed directly to the reader

    _____ other _____

2. What is the main idea of your composition?

    _____

    _____

    _____

    _____

3. What are three details that you use to support your main idea?

    _____

    _____

    _____

    _____

4. Does your composition have a clear beginning, middle, and end?

    Yes _____   No _____

5. Write down three examples of descriptive or interesting details that you used in your composition.

_____

_____

_____

_____

_____

6. What do you want your readers to learn from reading this composition?

_____

_____

_____

_____

7. How do you end your composition?

_____ summarize or restate the main idea

_____ address the reader directly

_____ make a prediction or comment on the future

_____ express an opinion

_____ express a thought, feeling, or statement related to the main idea

_____ leave the reader wondering about an unanswered question

_____ other _____

8. What are three possible titles for your composition?

_____

_____

_____

Topic 12:   Sleepwalker

Selena's English teacher asks her to write an expository composition in response to this prompt:

> What is sleepwalking? How does it happen? What are some of the common myths about sleepwalking and what is the truth behind those myths? Is sleepwalking dangerous? Who sleepwalks? Have you ever been a sleepwalker? Have you ever witnessed somebody sleepwalking? Write a composition telling what you know about this topic.

Here is one of Selena's drafts. Read it and then answer the questions that follow.

Selena's Draft A

Sleepwalking is a kind of sleep disorder where a sleeping person is doing activities like when they are awake. For example, they might get dressed, eat, go for walk, clean the house, or drive a car!

Most sleepwalking is short and perfectly harmless, although there are many myths out there that make sleepwalking sound worse and more frightening and disturbing than it really is. For example, in the movies, in plays, and on television, a sleepwalker usually has his arms out in front of him and his eyes closed. Not true. A sleepwalker will have his arms down by his side like as in normal, and he will have his eyes open (though they are not really seeing anything because their brains are asleep.) To bystanders, it may seem that the person is awake but however, if you look and study the person more closely, you will see that the eyes of a sleepwalker may appear blank. If you try to talk to someone who is sleepwalking, you may or may not get an answer. If the person does actually answer you, he might talk real slowly or not make any sense.

It has also been said that you should never wake up someone who is sleepwalking and this is not at all true either. Although a sleepwalker may be startled or confused if you wake him up, you can't actually do him any harm. In fact, waking a sleepwalker is sometimes the best thing to do, especially if that person is becoming a danger to himself or to others around him. Yes, it's true. And people can do some strange things when they are sleepwalking. Sleepwalkers have been known to eat, get dressed themselves, and even driven cars. Though rare, there have also been a number of times in which a sleeper has committed a crime. Are they guilty or not if they were sleeping? That's quite a dilemma for a judge. Others have accidentally hurt or killed themselves by stepping off balconies, falling down stairs or into pools or walking directly into traffic.

Despite there is no cure for sleeping, there is a whole lot of things that we do to keep a sleepwalker from hurting. Making sure that the sleeping person's bedroom is on the first or lowest floor is a great way to prevent any accidents on stairs or balconies.

(continued on next page)

(continued from previous page)

Keeping heavy drapes over windows and locking those windows is also a good idea. You want to be sure to keep the floor clear of objects or furniture that might become hazardous or unsafe even to a sleepwalker who is walking around in the middle of the night.

What it all really boils down to is that sleepwalking is something that can happen to anybody. People can do strange things while sleepwalking, even get hurt, so it is very important to keep them safe. If you have ever woken up with strange bruises that you have no recollection of getting, or woken up and found yourself to be doing something strange like getting dressed and three o'clock in the morning, then you might have been sleepwalking. Believe it or not, kids our age are the ones that it happens to most often!

1. How does the writer begin the composition?

    _____ a compelling or surprising fact

    _____ a thought-provoking question

    _____ an interesting quotation

    _____ a vivid description of an event

    _____ a sentence that states the main idea or topic

    _____ an opinion

    _____ a statement addressed directly to the reader

    _____ other _____

2. What is the main idea of the composition?

    _____

    _____

    _____

    _____

3. What are some details that support the main idea in this composition?

    _____

    _____

    _____

    _____

4. Is this composition well organized and easy to follow?   Yes _____   No _____

5. Descriptive details are details that help readers to get good pictures in their minds as they read. Underline five descriptive details in this draft.

6. A good composition has a clear beginning, middle, and end. Number the paragraphs in order as they occur. Tell which numbers are beginning paragraphs, which are middle paragraphs, and which are ending paragraphs.

_____

_____

_____

7. A good composition has varied sentence length to help with the flow. Write one example of a shorter sentence and one example of a longer sentence.

_____

_____

_____

_____

_____

_____

8. On a scale from 1 to 10, with 10 being the best, how would you rate this draft? Tell why.

_____

_____

_____

_____

9. How does the writer end the composition?

_____ summarizes or restates the main idea

_____ addresses the reader directly

_____ makes a prediction or comments on the future

_____ expresses an opinion

_____ expresses a thought, feeling, or statement related to the main idea

_____ leaves the reader wondering about an unanswered question

_____ other _____

Here is Selena's other draft. Read it and then answer the questions that follow.

Selena's Draft B

Have you ever woken up in the morning with strange bumps or bruises that you have no recollection of getting? Have you ever suddenly woken up in the middle of the night and found yourself getting dressed or eating a snack at the kitchen table? If so, you might have been sleepwalking. Sleepwalking is something that can happen to people of any age, but the highest rate occurs in people just on the verge of hitting their teens. That's you and me! Since this is something that could happen to any of us, it is best that we know exactly what it is and how to deal with it when and if it happens to us or to someone we know.

Sleepwalking is a kind of sleep disorder in which a sleeping person rises out of his bed and does things that he would normally only do when awake. Most incidents of sleepwalking are short-lived and perfectly harmless, although there are many myths that lead us to believe otherwise. A sleepwalker is typically portrayed as a person walking around like a zombie, with his arms out in front of him and his eyes closed. This, however, is not how it really happens. A sleepwalker's arms will be down by his side, and his eyes will be wide open. To bystanders, it may appear as though this person is actually awake. However, looking more closely, you will see that the eyes of a sleepwalker may appear glazed and empty. If you try to talk to someone who is sleepwalking, he may answer uncharacteristically slowly or be altogether unresponsive.

It has also been said that you should never wake up a person who is sleepwalking. This is not true either. Although a sleepwalker may be disoriented and confused when you wake him up, you can't actually do him any harm. In fact, waking a sleepwalker is sometimes the best thing to do, especially if that person is becoming a danger to himself or to others around him. Indeed, people can do some strange things when they are sleepwalking. Sleepwalkers have been known to have eaten, dressed themselves, and even driven cars. Though very rare, there have also been a number of instances in which sleepwalkers have committed terrible crimes. Others have accidentally hurt or killed

(continued on next page)

(continued from previous page)

themselves by stepping off balconies, tumbling down stairs, falling into pools, or walking directly into traffic.

Although there is no medical cure for sleepwalking, there are plenty of precautions that we can take to prevent a sleepwalker from getting hurt. Making sure that the person's bedroom is on the first floor is a great way to begin to prevent any accidents on stairs or balconies. Locking and draping heavy curtains over windows is also a good idea. Lastly, clear the floor of objects or furniture that might be hazardous to a sleepwalker who is wandering around aimlessly in the middle of the night.

It is important to remember that while sleepwalking is a disorder, nothing is actually wrong with a sleepwalker. As long as you do everything you can to keep the person safe, having a sleepwalker around can be a very interesting and even entertaining experience!

10. How does the writer begin the composition?

_____ a compelling or surprising fact

_____ a thought-provoking question

_____ an interesting quotation

_____ a vivid description of an event

_____ a sentence that states the main idea or topic

_____ an opinion

_____ a statement addressed directly to the reader

_____ other _____

11. What is the main idea of the composition?

_____

_____

_____

_____

12. Descriptive details are details that help readers to get good pictures in their minds as they read. Underline five descriptive details in this draft.

143

13. What are some details that support the main idea in this composition?

_____

_____

_____

_____

14. A good composition has a clear beginning, middle, and end. Number the paragraphs in order as they occur. Tell which numbers are beginning paragraphs, which are middle paragraphs, and which are ending paragraphs.

_____

_____

_____

15. Is this composition well organized and easy to follow?   Yes _____   No _____

16. A good composition has varied sentence length to help with the flow. Write one example of a shorter sentence and one example of a longer sentence.

_____

_____

_____

_____

17. On a scale from 1 to 10, with 10 being the best, how would you rate this draft?

_____

_____

_____

144

18. How does the writer end the composition?

_____ summarizes or restates the main idea

_____ addresses the reader directly

_____ makes a prediction or comments on the future

_____ expresses an opinion

_____ expresses a thought, feeling, or statement related to the main idea

_____ leaves the reader wondering about an unanswered question

_____ other _____

19. You have now read two drafts of Selena's work. One is the rough draft, and one is an improved draft.

Which do you think is the improved draft? Draft A _____   Draft B _____

20. Tell why you chose this draft.

_____

_____

_____

_____

_____

_____

_____

_____

_____

_____

_____

145

21. Rewrite the following sentence from Draft A so that it makes more sense.

Despite there is no cure for sleeping, there is a whole lot of things that

we do to keep sleepwalkers from hurting.

_____

_____

_____

_____

22. Write another possible introduction to this topic that uses a detailed description of a sleepwalker in action.

_____

_____

_____

_____

_____

_____

_____

_____

_____

_____

_____

_____

Now it's your turn. Write an expository composition in response to this prompt and then answer the questions that follow.

What is snoring? Who snores? Can snoring be dangerous or bad for the snorer's health? How can snoring negatively affect other people? Is there a cure for snoring? Write what you know about snoring. Try to use some humor, as well as descriptive details related to sound of snoring to make your composition particularly effective.

AS YOU WRITE YOUR COMPOSITION, REMEMBER TO:

- Begin the composition with a topic sentence.

- Choose at least three details to support your topic sentence.

- End with an idea that restates or pulls together the main topic or idea..

_____

_____

_____

_____

_____

_____

_____

_____

_____

_____

_____

1. How do you begin your composition?

_____ a compelling or surprising fact

_____ a thought-provoking question

_____ an interesting quotation

_____ a vivid description of an event

_____ a sentence that states the main idea or topic

_____ an opinion

_____ a statement addressed directly to the reader

_____ other _____

2. What is the main idea of your composition?

_____

_____

_____

_____

_____

3. What are three details that you use to support your main idea?

_____

_____

_____

_____

_____

4. Does your composition have a clear beginning, middle, and end?

Yes _____   No _____

5. Write down three examples of descriptive or interesting details that you used in your composition.

_____

_____

_____

_____

_____

6. What do you want your readers to learn from reading this composition?

_____

_____

_____

_____

_____

7. How do you end your composition?

_____ summarize or restate the main idea

_____ address the reader directly

_____ make a prediction or comment on the future

_____ express an opinion

_____ express a thought, feeling, or statement related to the main idea

_____ leave the reader wondering about an unanswered question

_____ other _____

8. What are three possible titles for your composition?

_____

_____

_____

To the Student: *Each of the last six assignments in this book asks you to read a rough draft of another student's work and then to rewrite it. Here are some things you can do to improve the rough drafts.*

- *Add interesting details.*
- *Add dialogue.*
- *Write well-organized paragraphs.*
- *Show emotions.*
- *Invent outstanding beginnings and endings.*
- *For further help, refer to **A Review: Good Writing** at the front of this book.*

Topic 13:   Daily News

Kisa's English teacher asks her to write an expository composition in response to this prompt:

> Many Americans read a newspaper on a daily basis. Tell what you think is the best way to go about reading the daily newspaper. Keep in mind that a newspaper can be very large and includes many different sections. Which section do you start with? Are there any sections that you recommend skipping? Which section do you most like reading?

This is Kisa's rough draft. As you read it, think about what you might like to improve.

Kisa's Rough Draft

Starting at the beginning, the front-page-section is the section where you would be likely to find the National and International news. You could read about wars and natural disasters and government information about the different countries in the world. This would be the place where you would find out what is going on the world and the country. You also would find the name of the newspaper, the date, the price, the index, the table of content, and the weather.

Then, in the next section, you might find your local news. That might be the kind of news where you might find out about what is going on in your town or surrounding towns. It might talk about what is happening in local town government, or where the new elementary school is going to be built, or what is going on this coming weekend at the town hall.

Then in the sports section, there would be scores and information about any big games that might have happened the day before in all sorts of sports like foot ball, baseball, basketball, soccer, golf, etc. They mainly might talk about sports from the whole country, not typically from the whole world. The only exception might be during the Olympics, which is the time when most of the countries in the world come together.

(continued on next page)

(continued from previous page)

Then there might be reports on world sports. Otherwise, aside from national and professional sporting news, there also might be sporting news about local high school and college sports.

Then in the business section comes news articles on any stories relating to business or money. In this secshun will also be the stocks and other information about how busyness around the country and the world are do-ing. After that, you might find an entertainment section. This is where you might have the comics, the television guide for the night, a list of movies that are playing nearby, and maybe some news articles on entertainment news like hollywood stars and musicians. This is also where there might be news about people getting married or people having babies, although some times that is in the local news section. It really depends on the newspaper.

The last section is usually the classified advertisement section. This is the section where people can buy and sell stuff like cars, furniture, pets, and other things. This is also the section where you could look for a job or a house or apartment. It's usually in the paper every single day, but on a weekend, they might make it a really big version of it or have a whole special section on real estate or cars or jobs.

You have read Kisa's rough draft. Can you improve it?

Please rewrite Kisa's composition here. Make sure you state the main idea at the beginning of the composition. Fix any spelling or grammatical errors that you see, clarify things that are confusing, remove sentences that you think don't belong, and add interesting details from your imagination.

_____

_____

_____

_____

_____

_____

_____

_____

_____

Now use your rewritten version of Kisa's rough draft to answer the following questions.

1. What is the main idea of your rewritten draft?

   _____

   _____

   _____

   _____

2. Name three details that you included to support the main idea.

   _____

   _____

   _____

   _____

3. Describe any problems that you saw in Kisa's draft.

   _____

   _____

   _____

   _____

4. How did you fix those problems when you rewrote it?

   _____

   _____

   _____

   _____

5. A good composition also has a clear beginning, middle, and end. Does yours have a clear beginning, middle, and end?

   Yes _____   No _____

6. A good writer tries to avoid run-on sentences and too many short, choppy sentences. He or she also tries not to use the same words over and over.

   In your rewritten draft, are all the sentences well written?   Yes _____   No _____

7. Descriptive details are details that give readers a picture in their minds as they read. Underline five descriptive details in your rewritten draft.

8. What do you want your readers to learn from reading this composition?

   _____

   _____

   _____

   _____

9. What do you like best about your rewritten composition? How is it better than Kisa's draft?

   _____

   _____

   _____

   _____

10. What are three other possible titles for your rewritten composition?

   _____

   _____

   _____

   _____

Topic 14:   Let's Dance

Max's English teacher asks him to write an expository composition in response to this prompt:

> What is dancing? Why do you think people dance? Why do some people enjoy dancing, while others don't? Why are there so many different types of dances, in accordance with different peoples and cultures?

As you read Max's rough draft, think about how you might like to improve it.

Max's Rough Draft

Dancing is something that people can do. It is a way of body movement. People like to dance because it's a liberating, freeing thing to move your body. Most of our days are spent following a routine. We go to school, we come home and do homework. We play a sport or participate in a club. We spend time on the couch watching television or sleeping. Dancing let's use let loose and be free. It's releases energy and makes you feel good. The people who don't like to dance maybe don't like to feel free like that. I think it's a good thing though.

There are so many different kinds of dances. Lots of them have been around for hundreds of years so we know that even back in the olden days, people danced. So even back then, people knew the benefits of dancing.

Probably, people started dancing way back when after music was invented. Dancing and music practically go hand in hand. Probably once music was invented, people couldn't help but move to the music. That is probably how dancing got started. There were a lot more structured dances back in time, but nowadays, people just sort of let loose and don't follow any sort of pattern. They just follow the music.

If you really like structured dancing, however, you can simply learn them. Most dances have certain steps or ways to do it. There are all sorts of types of ballroom dances. That is very classical. Like waltzes. There salsa dancing. There is flamenco dancing. There is ballet dancing. There is tap dancing and jazz dancing. There is the 50s and 60s styles of dancing like the jitterbug and the twist. Learning a real dance is actually fun because its neat to go through the steps. Country line dancing is fun. Square dancing is fun. The Electric Slide is fun. That's done at dances and weddings a lot. So is the Macarena.

There are so many kinds of dancing that everyone can find something that they like surely. If not, that's okay. Some people just don't like dancing. They like other things. It's just nice to have dancing as something that we can do if we want to do it. And lots of people take advantage of this and dance all the time. I know a family that turn the

(continued on next page)

(continued from previous page)

music on in their house every Friday night and dance like crazy until midnight. The whole family! Even the dog jumps up on his hind legs and dances. This is there special family time. So, you see, dancing can be great fun. It's entertaining to watch or to participate in. Take your pick.

You have read Max's rough draft. Can you improve it?

Please rewrite Max's composition here. Fix any spelling or grammatical errors that you see, clarify things that are confusing, remove sentences that you think don't belong, and add interesting details from your imagination.

_____

_____

_____

_____

_____

_____

_____

_____

_____

_____

_____

_____

_____

_____

Now use your rewritten version of Max's rough draft to answer the following questions.

1. What is the main idea of your rewritten draft?

   _____

   _____

   _____

   _____

2. Name three details that you included to support the main idea.

   _____

   _____

   _____

   _____

3. Describe any problems that you saw in Max's draft.

   _____

   _____

   _____

   _____

4. How did you fix those problems when you rewrote it?

   _____

   _____

   _____

   _____

5. A good composition also has a clear beginning, middle, and end. Does yours have a clear beginning, middle, and end?

   Yes _____   No _____

162

6. A good writer tries to avoid run-on sentences and too many short, choppy sentences. He or she also tries not to use the same words over and over.

    In your rewritten draft, are all the sentences well written?   Yes _____   No _____

7. Descriptive details are details that give readers a picture in their minds as they read. Underline five descriptive details in your rewritten draft.

8. What do you want your readers to learn from reading this composition?

    _____

    _____

    _____

    _____

9. What do you like best about your rewritten composition? How is it better than Max's draft?

    _____

    _____

    _____

    _____

10. What are three other possible titles for your rewritten composition?

    _____

    _____

    _____

    _____

Topic 15:   Shop 'Til You Drop

Ronald's English teacher asks him to write an expository composition in response to this prompt:

> A grocery store has numerous aisles that are filled with hundreds of thousands of items. What is the best way to do your food shopping for the week? How and where do you start? Do you make a list and then search for the items on that list? Do you simply walk up and down the aisles looking for what you need? In your opinion, what is the best, most efficient, and least time-consuming way to do the weekly food shopping?

Here is Ronald's rough draft. As you read, think about how you might like to improve it.

Ronald's Rough Draft

I like to start by making a store list at home. That way, I hopefuly won't be forgetting anything important. You can try to do your food shopping without a list, but it is really easy to forget something important. What you really should do is sit down with your family in your kitchen and look around and decide what you have and don't have and what you still need to buy.

Then what you need to do is take that list and go off to the store. You might want to go on a Sunday when all the coupons have come out in the Sunday newspaper because using coupons that you cut out of the paper is a really good way to save money. A lot of people use them. Then you will also see that when you get to the store, there will be some things on sale and while you're there, you might have to make some decisions.

So get to the store and you have to think where to start. I like to start with the items that don't need to be frigerated or frozen. The problem with that is you might take an hour to do your shopping, or sometimes more, and you don't want to have those frozen things sitting there the whole time obviously. They could melt.

So I start in the aisles for the cleaning products like soap and paper towels. Then I might do the pet food. Then I might do the unrefrigerated stuff like cereals and soups and boxes of stuff and cans of stuff and other stuff like that all. So I go up and down the aisles and make sure that while I do that I find every thing on my list as I go. Sometimes you have to look really carefully for stuff if you pass over it, you might get to the end of the aisles and have to go back, so look really carefully.

Then when you're all done with the dry goods, then you can go to the vegetables section, the deli section, the seafood section, the meat section, the milk and dairy section, and finally, last but not least, the frozen foods section. If you are gong to buy ice cream especially, do that last because it can really melt quick even though super markets are air conditioned.

(continued on next page)

164

(continued from previous page)

Some people like to cross things out as they go off their list. I do that if they're are a lot of things on my list. Otherwise however though I do not need to cross out. What I also like to do is to double check my list and make sure that I have gotten everything at all that I need. You definitely don't want to forget something, especially if you are doing the shopping for you parents and they have planned to make something for diner and you forget an ingredient.

The last thing of all that you do is to go to the checkout line and the cashier there will ring it all up and add it all up and tell you what your total is so that you know eexactly how much to pay him or her. Usually there is someone there to put all your stuff in bags too, but if not, you have to do it carefully. You shouldn't put cleaning products in with deli meat, for example. You never know what might break open in a bag. Also, don't put eggs or bread in the bottom of a bag that you then pack full of stuff. You don't want them to get squashed.

You have read Ronald's rough draft. Can you improve it?

Please rewrite Ronald's composition here. Make sure you state the main idea at the beginning of the composition. Fix any spelling or grammatical errors that you see, clarify things that are confusing, remove sentences that you think don't belong, and add interesting details from your imagination.

_____

_____

_____

_____

_____

_____

_____

_____

_____

_____

_____

Now use your rewritten version of Ronald's rough draft to answer the following questions.

1. What is the main idea of your rewritten draft?

    _____

    _____

    _____

    _____

2. Name three details that you included to support the main idea.

    _____

    _____

    _____

    _____

3. Describe any problems that you saw in Ronald's draft.

    _____

    _____

    _____

    _____

4. How did you fix those problems when you rewrote it?

    _____

    _____

    _____

    _____

5. A good composition also has a clear beginning, middle, and end. Does yours have a clear beginning, middle, and end?

    Yes _____   No _____

168

6. A good writer tries to avoid run-on sentences and too many short, choppy sentences. He or she also tries not to use the same words over and over.

   In your rewritten draft, are all the sentences well written? Yes _____   No _____

7. Descriptive details are details that give readers a picture in their minds as they read. Underline five descriptive details in your rewritten draft.

8. What do you want your readers to learn from reading this composition?

   _____

   _____

   _____

   _____

9. What do you like best about your rewritten composition? How is it better than Ronald's draft?

   _____

   _____

   _____

   _____

10. What are three other possible titles for your rewritten composition?

   _____

   _____

   _____

   _____

Topic 16:   Finishing the Job

Lourdes's English teacher asks her to write an expository composition in response to this prompt:

> What is the importance of finishing what you start? Is it ever okay to quit something before it's finished? Do you think that students nowadays are typically good at finishing activities and jobs that they start, or not? Many children and adults struggle with the concept of task completion. They move from one activity to the next without fully completing it. What could help them to become better task-completers? Use real-life examples to help support your composition on finishing the job.

As you read Lourdes's rough draft, think about how you might like to improve it.

Lourdes's Rough Draft

People definitely don't always finish what they start nowadays. Even students. Why? Who knows? People don't seem to take things as seriously anymore. For example, even kids who are playing a board game might just get totally bored and stop playing this game after twenty minutes. They might just throw it aside and go right into the next activity without really finishing it. Now, it would be different if it were the game of Monopoly that they were playing, because nobody can ever finish that game! But if it's just a game like Life or Trouble or something, they should finish it. It's good to finish things because it helps us to learn important lessons about finishing things.

The lesson is a good one. We can't become adults that don't complete things. Can you imagine that? Can you imagine if a teacher only taught half of a lesson and then stopped and then expected you to do a whole bunch of assignments on it? Can you imagine if your mom cooked your chicken dinner only halfway and then served it to you? Can you imagine if Steven Spielberg stopped directing a new blockbuster movie only part of the way through it? Can you imagine if builders only built half of a house? Can you see the importance of finishing the job? Imagine if you begged your parents for a dog and you finally got one, and then you decided that you didn't want one anymore. What would happen to the poor dog?

You might think that it is no big deal to not finish things like homework and school assignments. You might think that it is no big deal not to finish a book that you start reading or a tree house that you start building. You might think that it is no big deal not to finish decorating cookies after your dad buys you all the frosting and stuff for it. But finishing these things IS a big deal because it teaches this other more important lessons about responsibility for now and for our future lives. It also helps us to appreciate things. Definitely, finishing what we start is good and we should do it more often. Finishing what we start is so important. Otherwise, you might hear those two dreaded words made famous by Mr. Donald Trump, "You're Fired!"

170

You have read Lourdes's rough draft. Can you improve it?

Please rewrite Lourdes's composition here. Fix any spelling or grammatical errors that you see, clarify things that are confusing, remove sentences that you think don't belong, and add interesting details from your imagination.

Now use your rewritten version of Lourdes's rough draft to answer the following questions.

1. What is the main idea of your rewritten draft?

   _____

   _____

   _____

   _____

2. Name three details that you included to support the main idea.

   _____

   _____

   _____

   _____

3. Describe any problems that you saw in Lourdes's draft.

   _____

   _____

   _____

   _____

4. How did you fix those problems when you rewrote it?

   _____

   _____

   _____

   _____

5. A good composition also has a clear beginning, middle, and end. Does yours have a clear beginning, middle, and end?

   Yes _____   No _____

6. A good writer tries to avoid run-on sentences and too many short, choppy sentences. He or she also tries not to use the same words over and over.

   In your rewritten draft, are all the sentences well written?   Yes _____   No _____

7. Descriptive details are details that give readers a picture in their minds as they read. Underline five descriptive details in your rewritten draft.

8. What do you want your readers to learn from reading this composition?

   _____

   _____

   _____

   _____

9. What do you like best about your rewritten composition? How is it better than Lourdes's draft?

   _____

   _____

   _____

   _____

10. What are three other possible titles for your rewritten composition?

   _____

   _____

   _____

   _____

Topic 17:   Table Settings

Jamal's English teacher asks him to write an expository composition in response to this prompt:

> Imagine that your family is going to have a dinner party for ten people. All those people are going to need places to sit at a table and utensils to eat from. How many tables will you need? Do you have enough chairs? Once you have the table situation arranged, what happens next? When do you do the cooking? When do you put down the glasses, the silverware, the plates, the tablecloth, and the salt and pepper? Do you have enough room for the food and the condiments? Tell how you go about preparing for a dinner party of ten.

As you read Jamal's rough draft, think about how you might like to improve it.

Jamal's Rough Draft

What I do at the very start is that I make sure that I have enough room at my main table but I don't think so, at least not that much space for ten people so what I do is find some sort of folding table. If we don't have one, I will ask my neighbors because somebody must have a folding table that we can borrow if we promise to bring it back right after we're done. Then what I do is put the two tables right next to each other and I'll see if that enough space. It should be. After that, I start in cooking because that food needs to be in the oven for hours so that has to be done first.

Than I put on the tables cloths. Than the plates. Than the napkins and silverware or plasticware or whateverware you are eating with. I make sure that they are matching as best as possibility. I also make sure that they are all clean because it's kind of gross if someone finds a caked-on, dried up piece of food on a plate or a fork or something. They will be your guests so you want them to be comfortable and happy with the whole situation.

Then I put the glasses or cups on the table and the salt and pepper. If I need condiments like Tabasco sauce, ketchup, or mustard, or anything like that I will also put those on. Also salad dressing if you are serving a salad to the people. It totally depends on what is it that your eating. What you defanitely have to do is leave room for the food. Especially if you want to serve the food on the table and not in the kitchen. You have to make sure there is enough space to put the casserole dishes or bowls or platters or or whatever it is you are serving the food in.

Another thing you might like to do is put on some candles because candles always makes a dinner more elegant and pretty and people like to eat in candlelight. If you do not like candles, that is okay, just you regular lights. Also, another thing, if you have pets, make sure that they can stay away from the table. My cat sometimes tries to sneak

(continued on next page)

176

(continued from previous page)

on to the table. My dog some times chases the cat underneath the table and he can bang it and knock off all those items. The glasses are the thing to be most worried about because they could tip easier than anything else.

Another thing: You want serving spoons for the food that you are going to serve. What are people supposed to serve it up with if you don't give them serving spoons?

Once your table is set, you can go back to focusing on your dinner. Then greet your guests when they arrive and don't let them sit down at the table until dinner is served so that they don't mess anything up. Put them in the living room and give them an appetizer and a cold glass of lemonade, or hot tea or coffee, or whatever it is that they prefer while they are waiting. Then, when your dinner food is finally ready, that is the time to finally call them to the table and not before.

Don't forget that after your party, your work is not done. All those dishes will still be on your table and they can't just sit there or the leftover food will go bad and the dog will sneak up and try to get something. You must clean up after the guests. Sometimes the guests will offer to help, but not all the time and that is fine because they are guests. So you and whoever is helping you must bring in all those dishes and make sure the tables closthes are swiped down and finally, you can bring that other table back to your neighbor.

You have read Jamal's rough draft. Can you improve it?

Please rewrite Jamal's composition here. Make sure you state the main idea at the beginning of the composition. Fix any spelling or grammatical errors that you see, clarify things that are confusing, remove sentences that you think don't belong, and add interesting details from your imagination.

_____

_____

_____

_____

_____

_____

_____

_____

Now use your rewritten version of Jamal's rough draft to answe the following questions.

1. What is the main idea of your rewritten draft?

   _____

   _____

   _____

   _____

2. Name three details that you included to support the main idea.

   _____

   _____

   _____

   _____

3. Describe any problems that you saw in Jamal's draft.

   _____

   _____

   _____

   _____

4. How did you fix those problems when you rewrote it?

   _____

   _____

   _____

   _____

5. A good composition also has a clear beginning, middle, and end. Does yours have a clear beginning, middle, and end?

   Yes _____   No _____

6. A good writer tries to avoid run-on sentences and too many short, choppy sentences. He or she also tries not to use the same words over and over.

In your rewritten draft, are all the sentences well written?   Yes _____   No _____

7. Descriptive details are details that give readers a picture in their minds as they read. Underline five descriptive details in your rewritten draft.

8. What do you want your readers to learn from reading this composition?

_____

_____

_____

_____

9. What do you like best about your rewritten composition? How is it better than Jamal's draft?

_____

_____

_____

_____

10. What are three other possible titles for your rewritten composition?

_____

_____

_____

_____

181

Topic 18: United Branches of America

Stephen's English teacher asks him to write an expository composition in response to this prompt:

> There are three branches of government in the United States of America: the legislative, the judicial, and the executive. What are the responsibilities of each branch? How do they work together? Are any of the branches more important than the other? Tell what you know about the branches of government in our country from your experiences, observations, and studies.

As you read Stephen's rough draft, think about how you might like to improve it.

Stephen's Rough Draft

The legislative branch makes the laws and the big decisions related to the goings-on across our country. Although people have many differing positions and ideas about what might work best, the legislative branch tries to work together to come up with compromises that everyone can agree upon.

The judicial branch is made up of a system of federal courts that work hard to interpret, make sense of, and clarify the laws made by the legislators. The top court in the nation is the Supreme Court, which hears some of the most important cases in the country every day. It is the work of the judicial branch that makes it possible for the laws established by the legislative branch to be understood.

Once a law clearly clarified, the executive branch is then able to do its job: enforce the laws. The executive branch is not just comprised of the president and his cabinet, but of all the different departments: transportation, education, health and human services, homeland security, justice, treasury, among others. It is these departments that execute and enforce the laws.

What if the president of the United States suddenly decided to ban all citizens from driving their cars? What if congress suddenly decided that students must go to school seven days a week, three hundred sixty-five days a year, ten hours a day? What if the Supreme Court suddenly decided to assign the death penalty to any student who flunked a test or missed a day of school?

The United States of America has a special type of government that keeps such extreme scenarios from actually happening here. More than two hundred years ago, our founding fathers had the foresight and common sense to create a system of governing that makes sure that no one person or group has too much power. It's a simple and sensible system: the legislative branch makes the laws, the judicial branch interprets the laws, and the executive branch enforces them. None of the three main branches of government in this country is more or less important than the others.

182

You have read Stephen's rough draft. Can you improve it?

Please rewrite Stephen's composition here. Fix any spelling or grammatical errors that you see, clarify things that are confusing, remove sentences that you think don't belong, and add interesting details from your imagination.

184

185

Now use your rewritten version of Stephen's rough draft to answer the following questions.

1. What is the main idea of your rewritten draft?

    _____

    _____

    _____

    _____

2. Name three details that you included to support the main idea.

    _____

    _____

    _____

    _____

3. Describe any problems that you saw in Stephen's draft.

    _____

    _____

    _____

    _____

4. How did you fix those problems when you rewrote it?

    _____

    _____

    _____

    _____

5. A good composition also has a clear beginning, middle, and end. Does yours have a clear beginning, middle, and end?

    Yes _____   No _____

6. A good writer tries to avoid run-on sentences and too many short, choppy sentences. He or she also tries not to use the same words over and over.

In your rewritten draft, are all the sentences well written? Yes _____   No _____

7. Descriptive details are details that give readers a picture in their minds as they read. Underline five descriptive details in your rewritten draft.

8. What do you want your readers to learn from reading this composition?

_____

_____

_____

_____

9. What do you like best about your rewritten composition? How is it better than Stephen's draft?

_____

_____

_____

_____

10. What are three other possible titles for your rewritten composition?

_____

_____

_____

_____

Made in the USA
Columbia, SC
13 April 2024

34280183R00115